single HEARTED

Thirty Years of Service in Bangladesh

MARY LOU BROWNELL

Association of Baptists for World Evangelism
P.O. Box 8585
Harrisburg, PA 17105-8585
USA
(717) 774-7000
abwe@abwe.org
www.abwe.org

ABWE Canada
980 Adelaide St. South, Suite 34
London, Ontario N6E 1R3
(519) 690-1009
office@abwecanada.org

"Christ Our All in All" reprinted by permission of Louisiana State University Press from *The Complete Poems of Christina Rossetti, A Variorum Edition Volume II,* edited by R. W. Crump. Copyright © 1986 by Louisiana State University Press.

"The Lord's My Shepherd," *Scottish Psalter,* 1650; William Whittingham, et al., based on Psalm 23.

"When He Cometh," William Orcutt Cushing, 1823–1902, et al., based on Malachi 3:17.

Unless otherwise indicated, all Scripture quotations are taken from the *King James Version* of the Bible.

SINGLEHEARTED
  Thirty Years of Service in Bangladesh
Copyright © 2004 by ABWE Publishing
Harrisburg, Pennsylvania 17105

Library of Congress Cataloging-in-Publications Data (application pending)

Brownell, Mary Lou, 1929–
  Singlehearted
  Autobiographical, Non-fiction
  ISBN 1-888796-34-0 (Trade Paper)

All rights reserved. No portion of this book may be reproduced in any form without the written permission of the Publisher.

Printed in the United States of America.

*This book is dedicated to
all the missionary kids (MKs) I knew in Bangladesh.
They are gifted, flexible, courageous, and full of fun
and (slapstick) good humor. Their incredible ability to
make life on the mission field look like a walk in the
park cheered us immeasurably, no matter
how difficult the circumstances.*

*May God crown their lives with multiplied blessings
and use each of them to honor and glorify Him.*

Table of Contents

	Foreword	VII
	Acknowledgments	IX
	Prologue	XI
	Timeline	XV
	Maps	XVI
1	In the Beginning	1
2	Ichabod	9
3	Early Days	16
4	We Rest on Thee	24
5	Introduction to Third World Medicine	30
6	Consenting to Their Death	41
7	Faith Comes by Hearing	46
8	Overnight on a Salt Boat	51
9	The Roaring Lion	57
10	My Shepherd	64
11	Lesson from an Avocado Tree	68
12	Samaritan Woman	75
13	Our Extremity—God's Opportunity	85
14	Creepy Crawlies	92
15	Speaking of Angels	99
16	Called to Help	103
17	Cyclone!	107
18	How War Happened	114
19	Mountain Refuge	120
20	A Bittersweet Experience	128
21	A Day at the Beach	133
22	New Directions	138
23	Heart House	143
24	The Doll Lady—Prova's Story	150
25	Precious Jewels	157
26	A Fun Job	167
27	Acting Headmistress	175
28	A Perfect Gem	186
	Epilogue	191

Foreword

ABWE's single women always have held a special place of honor in my thinking. I have been challenged again and again by the dedicated lives and effective service of women such as Mary Lou Brownell.

I am delighted that she has preserved in writing many of her captivating experiences during her 28 years in Bangladesh (formerly East Pakistan).

A missionary must be a "jack of all trades." Mary Lou certainly was! Her training and talents were used by God in her roles as nurse, "dentist," school headmistress, creator and director of "Heart House," MK choir director and drama coach, and much more.

But God is more concerned about who a missionary is than what she does. The death of colleagues, devastating national disasters, civil war, and disappointments and trials all were used by the Lord to mold Mary Lou's life into an instrument which influenced the lives of missionary colleagues and nationals, both Bengalis and tribal people.

As Mary Lou's former administrator and then administrative colleague, it gives me great pleasure to recommend her fascinating story to you.

        Russell E. Ebersole
        Vice President of Missionary Ministries

Acknowledgments

Many people have been involved in making this book of memories possible. I'm grateful to North Baptist Church in Rochester, New York, my supporting/sending church. Pastor and people nurtured me from early childhood, encouraged my desire to serve in missions, and sustained me spiritually and financially through many years on the mission field.

My sister, Betty, and her husband, Bob, saved my correspondence from the field, allowing me to reach back into the distant past and write about events important to me. My family was extremely supportive, making room for me when I came home on furlough and cheering me on when I returned overseas.

Colleagues on the mission field became a "second family," and I'm thankful for the many years we served God together, learning a great deal about His goodness and grace. In essence, they are my story.

Those who read the manuscript (and laughed in all the right places) include: Becky Davey, Sheryl Jackson, Sheryl Liddle, Susan Nogle, and Carol Stagg. Their encouragement to keep writing spurred me on to finish the book.

Among those who prayed for me while I wrote and re-wrote were: Hazel Barrett, Reid Minich, Linda Nabors, and Arlina Robertson. It was a blessing to know they were praying, especially when words did not come easily and the necessary revision became tedious.

I could never have completed the manuscript without Kristen Stagg, friend, MK, author, and editor extraordinary. Kristen motivated me, smoothed my syntax, polished my prose, and (after all that) is still my friend.

Jeannie Lockerbie Stephenson, friend, missionary colleague, and author, remembered many details I had forgotten and gave much helpful advice.

Shirley Brinkerhoff, author, editor, and new-found friend, made the final editing and polishing a delightful experience for me with her sparkling creativity and enthusiasm.

Caroline Geier, research librarian at the Morgan County Library, Martinsville, Indiana, made her fingers fly on the computer until she found the source of the Christina Rossetti poem fragment used in the book.

I thank all of you who had a part in bringing this book to completion.

One note of explanation: most of the chapters in the book cover extended periods of time. When you read about Dacca, East Pakistan, and Dhaka, Bangladesh, in the same chapter, you haven't left one country and entered another. You have merely moved from pre-revolution (1971) East Pakistan to post-revolution Bangladesh.

Prologue

In March 1995, I was nearing the end of a six-month stint at Memorial Christian Hospital, in Malumghat, Bangladesh, and there were many farewell dinners in the homes of colleagues and Bengali friends. Prova, a close friend for many years, had invited me and several of my missionary co-workers to dinner. Ken James, the hospital maintenance man, drove our little group to Cha Bagan, the Christian village where Prova lives with her family.

In a Bengali home, conversation precedes dinner, so we sat and chatted with Prova and her kitchen helpers and admired her beautiful grandson first, then praised each dish as it was presented. The curry dinner, beautifully prepared and served, was well up to Prova's usual standard of excellence.

After dinner, we thanked our hostess for the wonderful food and her kindness in inviting us, then prepared to leave. She walked us partway to the car, then stopped suddenly in the middle of the path, gasped, and put her hand over her mouth. "Oh, no!" she wailed. "I forgot the most important thing. Please, Sister, come back to the house with me. I have a gift for you. I can't let you leave without it."

Ken and the others went on to the car while Prova and I walked quickly back to her mud-brick house. There, she retrieved a small box from the large wooden cupboard where she stores her valuables. Her hand trembled slightly as she placed the box in my hand. "Go ahead and open it," she urged.

I opened the small plastic jewelry box and gazed in astonishment. There, on a bed of crimson velvet, lay the loveliest ring I had ever seen in Bangladesh. A crystal-clear zircon was set in the center of a gold circlet. Tiny leaves, painstakingly formed from gold, decorated each side of the stone. The magnitude of Prova's gift was overwhelming; for a moment, speech failed me. "Oh, Prova, it's beautiful," I finally managed.

A widow, Prova is not a wealthy woman by any stretch of the imagination, and this was an extravagant gift. One of her grown sons, who had found work in the Middle East, was now home on leave and had helped Prova choose the stone and setting. I knew the ring had cost her dearly.

"Prova, I love it. I'll treasure it always. But why did you get it for me?"

"I wanted to give you something really precious," she said, her lovely eyes glistening with unshed tears. "I wanted it to be like Mary of Bethany's gift to our Lord. Sister, if God had not led you . . . if you had not come . . . we would have nothing. My family found Christ and a place in the church through your ministry. Now we have a home and my sons are educated. I had to find a way to thank God for sending you here and to thank you for coming." Still stunned, I thanked Prova, gave her a big hug, and walked out to the car, the sparkling ring gracing my finger.

Later, as I watched the light on the zircon explode into a brilliant rainbow, I felt I had come full circle in my adopted home. It was now many years since my arrival in East Pakistan in 1958, but in that time God had worked more miracles than I could count or remember. Prova is only one of those grace stories, a precious jewel in her own right.

Heart House, a ministry that trains women to support themselves, and the project in which Prova was involved, had been my "baby." I had planned and brought it to birth, with a great deal of assistance, after the grim events of the country's civil war in 1971. Many women, either widowed or abandoned as war swept through the country, were left totally destitute, and Prova was one of them. She had been a vital part of the Heart House ministry from its earliest days, and she had continued her work there even after I left Bangladesh and other missionaries faithfully carried on the work, pulling Heart House through difficult, lean times.

Today, God continues to extend His grace through new missionary colleagues, who still tell the same old, old story of His love. God's intervention in the lives of Bengali people spans the more than 40 years of ABWE's history in the exotic, tragic land of Bangladesh. And what wonderful stories they are! If God had not intervened in *our* lives—if He had not sent us to serve with single hearts and a common goal—if we had not gone—these grace stories never would have happened, and I never would have met Prova and all the others, nor seen what God could do in their lives.

Timeline

1957	Millers and Barnards go to Chittagong, East Pakistan.
April 1958	Gurganuses, Canfields, and Mary Lou Brownell arrive in East Pakistan.
June 1958	Riot/stoning at Tabernacle. Khoka is saved.
February 1960	Joyce Wingo and Mary Lou move to Hebron.
August 1960	Gene Gurganus returns to the U.S.
September 1960	The Jay Walsh family moves to Hebron.
October 1961	Mary Lou moves to Chittagong.
January 1962	The Vic Olsen family arrives in Chittagong.
October 1963	Work begins on Memorial Christian Hospital in Malumghat. Becky Davey and Mary Lou move into an apartment with Shabi.
1963	The Harry Goehring family arrives on the field.
June 1965	Harry Goehring dies.
September 1965	War with India. Becky and Mary Lou, on vacation, are caught outside the country for over two months.
March 1966	Dedication of Memorial Christian Hospital at Malumghat.
January 1967	Mary Lou moves to hospital and begins work as Matron.
December 1967	Cholera epidemic at Malumghat.
April 1971	Civil War breaks out between West Pakistan and newly formed Bangladesh. Gwen, Linda, and Mary Lou go to West Pakistan to stay in Quetta with Hollands. They return to Bangladesh about six weeks later.
1972	Heart House begins operations.
1981	Mary Lou takes over management of Malumghat Christian School.
1985	Mary Lou leaves the field.

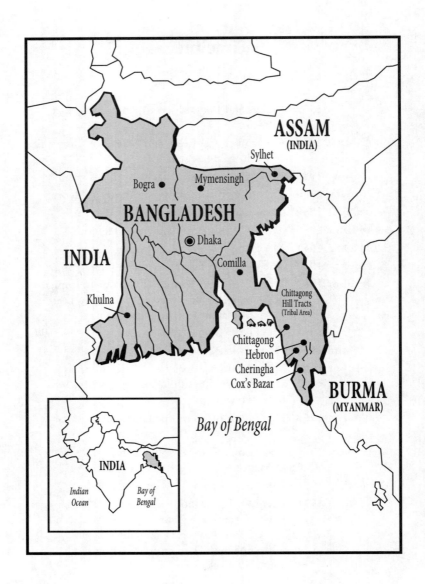

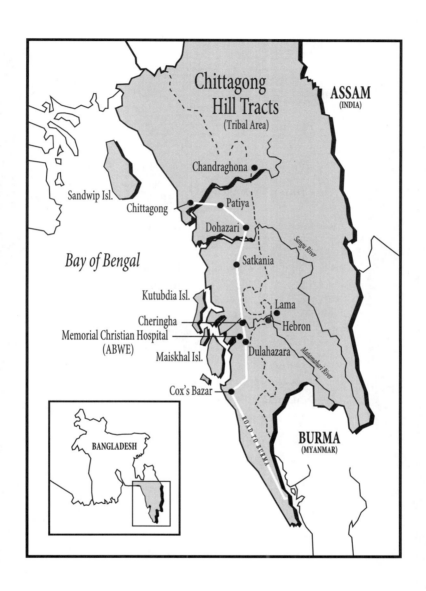

CHRIST OUR ALL IN ALL

Lord, what have I that I may offer Thee?
Look, Lord, I pray Thee, and see.

Nay, child, what is it thou has not?
Thou hast all gifts I have given to thee:
Offer them all to me,
The great ones and the small,
I will accept them one and all.

I have a will, good Lord, but it is marred;
A heart both crushed and hard:
Not such as these the gift
Clean-handed lovely saints uplift.

Nay, child, but will thou judge for me?
I crave not thine, but thee.

Ah, Lord, who lovest me!
Such as I have now give I Thee.

—*Excerpted from "Christ Our All In All"*
  Christina Georgina Rossetti (1830–1894)

one

In the Beginning

I was the first in my family to be born in the United States, but my roots are planted deep in Canadian soil. My ancestors moved to Canada from England, Ireland, and Scotland, and my three older siblings were born there. After my family moved to the United States, my younger brother, Stan, and I were born in Rochester, New York. Canadian relatives loved to call us "Yankee." They thought it was funny, but I didn't like being different from my older siblings, even though I was fiercely American and proud that I had been born in the U.S.A.

I have learned to appreciate my Canadian heritage. My father, Stanley Brownell, came from Moulinette, a small town in eastern Ontario. Among the Brownells in our history were artists, teachers, and preachers, many of whom had a deep faith in God and a work ethic that would stand them in good stead for generations to come.

Once, while visiting my father's relatives in Cornwall, Ontario, I asked Aunt Hilda how my mother, Muriel Pettit, met my father. "He was traveling west with the railroad," she explained, "and the workers stopped in a lot of small towns along the way, including the one where your mother lived. Your father's brother, Bruce, met your Aunt Vera the same way." Eventually, my father and mother, Uncle Bruce and Aunt Vera, along with my mother's sister, Ada, and her family, emigrated to western New York.

I appreciate the dedication of my parents. It is a tribute to them that I cannot remember ever being cold or hungry, even in the lean days of the Depression. My father worked as a contractor and always kept busy. Looking back, I guess we were poor, but that never occurred to me at the time. My brother Walt and sister Betty found employment; Nina, Stan, and I were still in school. Ours was a big family to feed, clothe, and house. It could not have been an easy task, but my parents managed on limited resources and graced their children with traditional values and a sincere faith in God.

We were a noisy, fun-loving bunch of kids. Mother was a stern disciplinarian and administered swift justice to the guilty—and sometimes to the innocent—which undoubtedly helped keep us under control. All of us inherited Mother's love of beauty. She would have enjoyed beautiful clothes and a home of her own, but sacrificed many things that would have enriched her life to provide the things we children needed.

She also had a delightful sense of humor, and she was an excellent seamstress and a good cook. When young people gathered at our house for the evening, they always ended up in the kitchen with her. My sisters and I still talk about the foods Mother cooked, baked, and preserved.

Dad was a quiet man with a twinkle in his eye. He was short, so his buddies nicknamed him "Stubby." A jack-of-all-trades, he was willing to turn his hand to almost any project. When he worked for the railroad in Canada, he had been a cook, so it was natural that he often made Sunday morning breakfast for the family: fried eggs, crisp bacon, and Parker House rolls that we still fondly remember.

Dad used his capable hands until Parkinson's disease took away his ability to handle tools. He suffered a series of heart attacks and died a few months before I finished nurse's training. It was hard to lose him, but disease had reduced him to a mere shadow.

Mother was emotionally strong, so it's not strange that she raised strong sons and daughters. Both parents used their hands skillfully, so it is not surprising that all of us enjoy art, music, crafts, and gardening. Walt, the oldest child, had bulbar polio as a young boy, and the doctor did not hold out much hope for his recovery. "If you send him to the hospital, he'll die," the doctor said. "If you keep him at home and watch him closely, he has a chance." Mother and Dad nursed Walt around the clock until he recovered.

Mother had to be strong again when Walt went to war. He was still a Canadian citizen when the United States entered World War II. He crossed the border and joined the Royal Canadian Air Force. Walt participated in some of the worst bombing raids over Germany and had several close calls, so we were thankful when he returned home safely.

Mother sent us to North Baptist Church, a small neighborhood church blessed with pastors who loved the Lord and faithfully taught God's Word. I still remember the bronze sign on its lawn that said "Fundamentalist." I heard the gospel from the time I was very small, and I knew that Jesus Christ was God's Son, that He came to earth to die on the cross for my sins, that He rose from the dead, and that He would some day return to earth and take those who love Him to live in heaven forever. John 3:16 became very special to me when a Sunday school teacher showed me how to insert my name in the Bible verse: "For God so loved *Mary Lou* that he gave his only begotten Son, that if *Mary Lou* believeth in him she should not perish, but have everlasting life." I accepted Jesus Christ as my Savior at a Bible club rally when I was ten years old. Mrs. Betlem, the pastor's wife, smiled and said, "Mary Lou, I'm glad you accepted Christ as your Savior today. I've been praying for you for a long time."

Pastor John Betlem led the church for much of my life. He was born in the Netherlands and loved the sea. His greatest delight was sailing his small boat on Lake Ontario. He also loved to look at the starry sky through his telescope. He was a fiery preacher, somewhat intimidating in the pulpit, but he gave me a solid foundation in the Bible and an awe of God's majesty that has stayed with me throughout my life.

North Baptist Church's great interest in missions had a lasting impact on my life. Bob and Grace Kohler left to serve with The Association of Baptists for World Evangelism (ABWE) in the Philippines shortly before World War II. I was only about twelve years old, but I still have a vivid mental picture of the excited young couple as they prepared to leave home, and of the congregation's excitement at sending out "home-grown" missionaries.

The church family followed the Kohlers' career closely, and was shocked and distressed when they disappeared suddenly. The Japanese imprisoned missionaries in the Philippines after Pearl Harbor, but no one had any information about Bob and Grace.

The Kohlers suddenly reappeared almost four years later. Rather than give themselves up to the Japanese, they had fled to the hills of Mindanao, where Filipino Christians protected them at great personal risk. General Douglas MacArthur's advance party found the Kohlers and took them to Australia by submarine. I remember their first visit to our church when they returned to the United States. Bob and Grace were thin and weary, and daughters Joyce and Lou Anne were like little gazelles, ready to flee at the first sign of danger. They had been through some harrowing experiences, but God had protected and brought them back to us. This was a wonderful testimony to God's faithfulness, and a good lesson for anyone interested in pursuing missions as a career.

Reading missionary biographies and listening to missionary experiences also helped point me toward career missions. Inborn genes may have a great deal to do with the strengths, weaknesses, gifts, and talents passed from generation to generation, but God is the One who puts the pieces together in a way that best accomplishes His perfect will.

I worked for a year after high school, then headed off to Baptist Bible Seminary, in Johnson City, New York, where my sister Nina and her husband, Ben, were training for missionary service. My oldest sister, Betty, and her husband had already graduated from BBS, and Bob was preparing for military service as a chaplain.

I studied in the missions program at BBS for four years. I had to pay my own expenses, so I became an entrepreneur, ironing men's shirts several afternoons each week. I lived in a house with five other girls, fellow students at BBS. Study, work, and kitchen chores consumed most of our time, but our cooperative efforts taught us to live happily together and to use our limited resources wisely. I graduated debt-free, an exercise in daily dependence upon God.

He often met a need at the last possible moment. I took ten cents from my tithe bank one evening because I thought I might have to catch a bus home after prayer meeting. It was still light enough to walk to church, but it would be dark and much colder by the time I started back. A friend offered me a ride home, and I sheepishly put the dime back in my bank.

Another time, Nina and Ben sent me a check. Usually, when a check arrived, Nina and Ben told me to divide the money with Homer, who was Ben's brother and a fellow student at BBS. This particular check, however, was exactly the amount I needed to pay a school bill. I cashed the check, tracked down Homer, and said, "Homer, here's your half of the money Nina and Ben sent." He laughed and said, "Keep it. I got a check just like it. This money is all yours." I was overwhelmed with God's—as well as Ben's and Nina's—goodness. They were raising funds to go to Africa with Baptist Mid-Missions, but they still shared what they had with me. Experiences such as this assured me that God would continue to provide for me as I learned to trust Him.

In 1952, Baptist Bible Seminary was trying to obtain New York State accreditation. I left BBS at the end of my fourth year, even though I had almost enough credits to obtain my degree. God was speaking to me about nurse's training, something that seemed like an impossible dream. I had no way to finance training of any kind, but the Lord continued to nudge me in that direction.

If I studied nursing in a state psychiatric hospital, New York State would cover my expenses. But I really did not want to study nursing in a mental hospital. God graciously opened the door for me to train instead at Highland Hospital, close to my family and home church. I passed the entrance exam and was invited to join the nursing class of 1955.

If I thought BBS was a challenge, nurse's training beat it by miles! Our director was definitely "old school." Fortunately, some of our clinical instructors were young, friendly, and helpful. As students, we were not allowed to hum, chew gum, whistle, run, or remove any part of our uniform until we were off the residence hall's main floor. By the time we hit the third floor—running—we were out of uniform and ready to change into comfortable clothes.

If we arrived back at the dorm close to duty time, we learned to change back into uniform in three minutes flat. This may sound like a simple exercise, but our uniforms were stiff with starch. We had to peg collar and cuffs into slots with tiny plastic studs and button stiff apron straps into tiny buttonholes. Our white shoes, shoelaces, and hose had to be scrupulously clean. We wore our hair above the collar and secured our stiff, starchy caps with bobby pins. Rings or earrings of any kind were forbidden. I am still shocked when I walk into my doctor's office and see nurses wearing brightly colored running shoes.

During my last year in training, I again faced the question, "What does the Lord have in mind for me?" Ginny Forkell, a childhood friend working with ABWE in Chile, sent me an article about ABWE's survey team, which was visiting East Pakistan to determine the feasibility of a new work there. I kept the article in mind, but I knew it would be several months before results of the survey reached me.

I graduated from nurse's training in 1955 and returned to Baptist Bible Seminary to complete my Th.B. degree. By this time, Baptist Bible Seminary (now Baptist Bible College) was fully accredited by New York State. I was able to transfer liberal arts credits from nurse's training, and I had already completed most of the other course work, so I finished my Th.B. in one year while gaining nursing experience at Wilson Memorial Hospital in Johnson City at the same time.

Because I was one of the few nurses with experience in communicable diseases, I was assigned to the polio ward. Children received the Salk vaccine for the first time that summer, but the ward was full of desperately ill patients. We ran our legs off carrying steaming hot packs—the only treatment that would soothe their terrible muscle spasms. Some of us also nervously awaited the results of our nursing State Boards, and it was a happy day when I learned that I had become a full-fledged registered nurse.

Later that year, my friend Ginny told me that ABWE had made the decision to begin the new work in East Pakistan. I was drawn more and more toward this new mission field. Two couples were preparing for service there: Victor and Winnifred Barnard, Australians with considerable missionary experience in East Bengal; and Paul and Helen Miller, who had decided to help the Barnards pioneer the new work.

When Mr. Barnard spoke eloquently at BBS about East Pakistan and its needs, I felt God wanted me on their team. I applied to ABWE and was invited to attend missionary training classes in September 1956.

ABWE held candidate classes at their lovely Germantown, Pennsylvania, mission house. Candidates spent four weeks studying the policies, practices, and history of the mission. We did chores, helped with meals, sang, prayed, studied together, and became a close-knit family. Missionaries on furlough gave fascinating reports, showed slides, and answered our endless questions.

By the time candidate classes ended, we were all highly motivated to minister in the place of God's choosing.

During candidate classes, I spent time with Ruth Woodworth and Mona Kemery, single women missionaries who had been imprisoned by the Japanese in World War II. In spite of all they had suffered, they were attractive, humorous, intelligent women who had cheerfully left home, family, and marriage prospects to serve God overseas. They greatly encouraged the single women in the class and assured us that we could serve God happily and effectively.

At the end of classes, Gene and Elizabeth (Beth) Gurganus, nurse Juanita Canfield, and I were appointed to East Pakistan. I returned home to begin raising the prayer and financial support I needed to serve the Lord in East Pakistan.

I spent eighteen months raising travel funds and monthly support—just $250 at that time. Most of my financial support came from small country churches, and $20 a month from such churches was a munificent gift. I praised God for every dollar that brought me closer to departure.

In March 1958, I left Rochester in a snowstorm and took a train to Philadelphia, where I met the Gurganuses and Juanita Canfield at the ABWE mission house. We then traveled to New York City, intending to board the Greek freighter that would take us to East Pakistan, but our departure was delayed for several days because of the storm. My sister Betty, her husband, Bob, and my mother came to New York to see me off when we finally sailed out of New York Harbor on that frigid March day. I had never been farther away from home than Canada. This was a journey into unknown waters.

t w o

Ichabod

The ship on which we sailed was a Hellenic Lines freighter called the *Glory*. Whenever he talked about our departure, Gene Gurganus loved to use the Hebrew word *Ichabod,* then grin gleefully and interpret from the Bible: "the Glory has departed." Two young businessmen and a woman celebrating her retirement with a trip to Greece sailed with us, so there were eight passengers in all.

The ship had a flexible schedule, to say the least. No one seemed to know how long it would take to reach East Pakistan, or where the crew might be asked to pick up cargo along the way. During our trip across the Atlantic, the crew's immediate goal was Piraeus, Greece, which is close to Athens. Piraeus was their home port, and every inch of the ship had to be cleaned and painted to prepare the *Glory* for its triumphal return.

While on board, we learned to eat eggs scrambled in olive oil, rice steamed in grapevine leaves, and other delicious Greek dishes. I had come through college and nurse's training without succumbing to the allure of brewed coffee. Now I fell in love with a thick, sweet brew called *kafedis,* finely ground coffee and water boiled three times in a special copper pot before being poured into tiny cups. *Kafedis* is the equivalent of Turkish coffee, and one small cup will keep you awake for hours. I found it hard to resist.

Throughout our journey, Captain Macris talked about World War II as though it had just happened. Listening to his stories, the war in Greece became very real to us. The captain had joined the merchant marine at the beginning of the war, afraid of what might be required of him if he remained at home. "I left my wife and children in Athens when I went to sea, and I feared for their lives every moment I was away," he said. "I knew food was scarce, and my wife had no way of getting money. I sent gold coins to her with any mariner friends I knew were going back to Athens."

His wife gave birth to their daughter after his departure, and Captain Macris didn't even learn the baby's name until he returned home after the war. He laughed as he told us, "My wife put our daughter's name in letters several times, but the censors always cut it out, thinking she was communicating sensitive information by code. I was really frustrated."

I had always thought that only those Jews living in the countries close to Germany were marked for extermination in World War II, but Captain Macris told us that thousands of Jews in other places were also slaughtered during the war, hounded to death even in countries such as Greece.

Although we left the U.S. in early spring, our northern route across the Atlantic, via the Azores, proved stormy indeed. Beth was seasick most of the time. Juanita and I bundled up and braved the deck. After a few days of queasiness, we began to enjoy the long days at sea. The *Glory* skimmed the green, wild coast of Portugal before reaching the milder Mediterranean climate and calmer seas. We marveled at flying fish, dancing dolphins, and the emerald, phosphorescent wake of the *Glory* at night. It was an exciting new world, and we reveled in its beauty. At last we steamed proudly into Piraeus with flags flying. The sailors were exuberant, eager to see their families. Most of the crew took off for home as quickly as possible.

Athens is just a bus ride from the port of Piraeus, so we disembarked to explore. I was unprepared for the exquisite beauty of the Greek capital, which looked as though it had existed forever. The city was ours to enjoy as we walked in the footsteps of the apostle Paul, seeing the same sights he must have seen almost two millennia before. We were greatly impressed by the city's cleanliness and the casual approach its citizens take to life. We soon learned that city businesses close at 1:00 p.m. and everyone goes home to eat lunch with the family and rest through the heat of the day. During this time, we couldn't find any restaurant or shop open for business. Late in the afternoon, the city wakes up and returns to work, staying open until well into the evening. Athenians enjoy a late dinner hour, and it was hard for us to become accustomed to eating dinner at 9:00 or 10:00 p.m. Instead, we strolled through markets, sampling the Greek food in small cafés and street stalls.

• • •

We loved every moment in Athens but were eager to continue on to East Pakistan. While sailing through the Suez Canal, we caught a brief glimpse of Egypt. I'm sure the wonders of that country are marvelous, but Port Said is not a fitting introduction. Our experience of this first truly Eastern port left us unimpressed. We were glad to get back on board the *Glory*, among people we knew and trusted.

One day on ship, we were sure we had lost 4-year-old Lydia Gurganus. We searched frantically, up and down the passageways, in and out of cabins. Had she fallen overboard? Freighters make no special arrangements for children, and it would be easy for a child her size to slip between the railing bars into the sea.

Then we heard a familiar giggle. We followed the sound and found tiny, blond Lydia sitting on the table in the officers' wardroom. She was blissfully entertaining a group of off-duty officers with her southern accent. We breathed a sigh of relief and made a mental note to keep sharper eyes on this fearless mite. The ship was her home, and she wandered the passageways without a care in the world.

We stopped briefly in Karachi, West Pakistan, to unload cargo. More than ten years had passed since an act of British parliament created the Muslim nation of Pakistan, divided into East and West Pakistan and separated from one another by India. Yet the port of Karachi amply displayed the ravages of that violent partition. Our time in port was limited, but we were haunted for a long time after by the stark images we saw there. Mothers holding pale, listless babies in their arms sat along the streets, begging with outstretched, claw-like hands. It was the first time I had seen such appalling need, and I was horrified. The crew was no help at all. "You think Karachi is bad," they said, "wait until you see Chittagong. It's even worse!"

I had picked up a virus along the way and was feeling wretched. My head pounded, and I ached all over. My physical condition mirrored my emotional misery precisely. How could I live in a place worse than Karachi? The first mate, sensing my turmoil, said, "Don't worry. If you don't like it in Chittagong, we'll be happy to take you home again!" That was not exactly what I had in mind, nor an option I wanted to consider.

One day Captain Macris told us, "Our office in New York has sent word that the *Glory* might not stop in Chittagong. We may have to trans-ship the Chittagong cargo, and leave you wherever we unload it." We had visions of being abandoned, baggage in hand, and having to find our way to Chittagong from who knows where. Wouldn't *that* be fun? I'm sure Gene was the one with nightmares! He probably imagined himself left on a dock, surrounded by a mountain of luggage, responsible for the care and safety of four females.

We stopped briefly in Ceylon (now Sri Lanka) and spent a little time exploring its capital, Colombo. It was tropical, rainy, and perfumed with flowers. It was good to walk on land again, even if only for a few hours. In Colombo, Captain Macris received permission to unload cargo in Chittagong. That was a huge relief, and we began to make preparations to leave the ship.

Recent heavy storms in the area meant Chittagong harbor was full of ships waiting to unload when the *Glory* arrived. Since ships are berthed in port in the order in which they arrive, our ship had to wait at outer anchorage for its turn to enter the harbor. Several days passed as we languished there. Concerned ship's officers kept asking, "Are you sure you really want to stay here? Don't you want us to take you back to New York?" But by this time, we were so eager to see our new homeland and co-workers that we could hardly wait to get off the ship!

At last Captain Macris announced, "Your people in Chittagong have asked permission for you to leave the ship and go into port with the pilot boat, which should be here within the hour. You need to get your stateroom luggage. We'll unload everything else once we're in port."

You would have laughed at our departure from the ship, although it didn't seem funny at the time. Gene and some of the crew loaded our cabin luggage into the bottom of a small boat, which bobbed vigorously beside the *Glory* in the swelling waves. The rest of us had to climb down the gangway, transfer to a metal ladder, then drop into the boat at the exact moment the boat crested on the waves. Somehow, we all made it safely, and the small boat carried us to the waiting pilot boat.

Lydia screamed her terror the entire way. Her cries of "We're sinking! We're sinking!" rang in our ears for a long time. Beth tried to calm her by assuring the toddler, "It's all right, Lydia. It's all right. We're not going to sink. We're almost there." But we were not absolutely sure Lydia was wrong. Our transfer to the pilot boat was smoother. The motor-powered launch, considerably larger than the transfer boat, was easier to clamber into and proved to be much more comfortable.

What we did not know was that the pilot boat would follow its appointed rounds before taking us to our destination. It stopped at almost every ship in harbor, checking official papers, delivering mail, and doing its customary jobs for several hours. We had no food or water with us, because we had assumed that our trip to shore would be brief. When Captain Macris visited us later and heard what had happened, he was aghast. "I am so sorry. I had no idea they would do that to you," he stormed. "If I had known you'd be on the boat all day, I would have sent food and water with you." We felt most sorry for poor Lydia. It was a hot day, and we didn't have a drop of water to give the thirsty little girl.

Hours later, the pilot boat docked next to several barges. We walked across the barges and a narrow strip of grass and finally entered East Pakistan! Two cars roared up, disgorging the Millers and the Barnards, who greeted us like long-lost family. Hot, bedraggled, thirsty, hungry, and weary, we had reached the end of our journey.

Victor and Winnifred Barnard took us into the customs shed for baggage inspection, while Paul and Helen Miller hurried off to find food and water. They returned a bit later with banana cake from the *bazar* and fresh, drinkable water. These refreshed us for baggage inspection, which proved to be only a cursory examination before the customs officers waved us through the barriers. (The real inspection came weeks later when the *Glory* unloaded our trunks and metal 55-gallon drums into the customs warehouse. Negotiating a settlement with customs officials would last weeks, while mosquitoes feasted on our limbs and perspiration ran down our necks and burned in our eyes.)

We climbed into the vehicles and headed into Chittagong. Juanita and I were to stay with Victor, Winnifred, and their young daughter, Lauranne, until we could move into our own apartment. Until an apartment was ready for them, the Gurganuses would share the Miller home. It was almost evening by the time Juanita and I reached the Barnards' home. Nothing I had seen thus far looked as terrible as Karachi. Perhaps Chittagong wasn't so bad after all.

We were exhausted after our long day and eager to stretch out and rest, but Juanita and I made some interesting discoveries that short-circuited any thought of a restful night. Winnifred carefully showed us how to tuck in the mosquito nets that draped our beds. For some reason, however, the nets did not keep the mosquitoes out. I would drift off, only to hear Juanita slap at a mosquito. The next morning we discovered that our thin mattresses were supported by heavy strapping that crisscrossed the wooden bed frame. Mosquitoes came up between the strapping and the mattress in places the nets didn't cover. I think more mosquitoes ended up inside the nets than outside!

Another problem remained unidentified until morning. The Barnard house was close to the road, but there were few motorized vehicles in those days. However, something repeatedly whizzed by the house, making a noise like a bicycle bell. What could it possibly be? Victor told us our arrival fell during Ramazan, the Muslim month of fasting, when Muslims may eat and drink only between sundown and sunrise. During this month, they sleep as much as possible during the day, working and shopping after sundown when it's cooler. Bicycle rickshaws are a common form of transportation for such tasks, designed to carry several passengers from place to place day or night, and it was the sound of these rickshaws whizzing past the house, bells clanging loudly, which kept Juanita and me awake on our first night in Chittagong.

We learned that commerce slows to a crawl during Ramazan. Since every piece of furniture Juanita and I would need had to be made in the small shops near the Barnard home, it was slow work furnishing our apartment and gathering what we would require for housekeeping. Government offices keep especially short hours during the month of fasting, and it took weeks to claim our baggage and have it delivered.

Captain Macris visited us before the *Glory* left Chittagong. "Are you sure," he inquired kindly, "that you don't want me to take you back to America? There's room for you on the ship, you know." We thanked him for his offer, but we had reached the place of God's choosing, and—for the moment—that was sufficient.

three

Early Days

Each term in a missionary's life possesses its own unique character. It may be easy or extremely difficult, depending on a kaleidoscope of circumstances over which the missionary has no control. What holds a missionary steady is the firm belief that, while life may seem to be spinning out of control, in reality God controls every situation and knows exactly what He is doing.

Looking back on those first years in East Pakistan, I believe they were the most difficult of the nearly three decades I lived in the country. I do think, however, that we missionaries who arrived in the early days had it easier than those who came later. We who pioneered ABWE's mission work in East Pakistan came from backgrounds of economic poverty. We had lived through the Depression as children; our expectations were limited to sufficient warm clothes, a roof over our heads, and food on the table. We had experienced gasoline and food rationing during World War II, and we were grateful that the little we owned was adequate for our basic needs. The economic level from which we came was closer to that of the Bengali people, although still light years apart, since we were never exposed to starvation, disease, and extreme poverty as many Bengalis were.

Missionaries who arrived in later years came from a strong, post-war economy and a more prosperous lifestyle, to a country that had changed very little since its birth in 1947. Change is rapid in the West, but slow in the East. Thus, the eons of separation between missionary and national—in ideology, economics, science, and technology—increased, rather than decreased.

To be effective in ministry, anyone working on a mission field where the language, culture, and standard of living differ greatly from his own must find ways to bridge the gaps created by these differences. New missionaries must learn to cope with the challenges that bombard them from the moment they step on foreign soil.

Perhaps my greatest shock was the realization that I didn't really *want* to change in order to adjust to this new culture. I enjoy being American; I like my white skin; I'd rather speak English than Bengali. Recognizing and conquering each rebellious preference and prejudice takes a long time and is a slow, often painful, struggle. If a missionary is to survive, thrive, and minister effectively in his adopted country, he must win this first battle before defeat renders him powerless.

As a new missionary in East Pakistan, I had to settle in and learn to keep house. Juanita and I lived in an apartment building called Hamza Mansion, which was far from most people's idea of a mansion. The building boasted 12 two-bedroom apartments, four on each floor. Winnifred Barnard, who knew the language and had spent many years in East Bengal, did most of her own cooking and cleaning. Juanita and I, however, would spend many hours in language study and needed household help to make that possible. Mr. Barnard hired a houseboy (called a bearer) to help us with marketing, cooking, and laundry. The bearer had no training in household care, however, so Juanita and I tried to teach him basic cooking and cleaning. Considering the language barrier and our lack of knowledge about local food markets, it's amazing that we were able to impart anything to him.

While living in Chittagong, Juanita and I learned to cook what was available in the local market, even managing to fix some dishes that looked and tasted almost American. Many years later, missionaries were able to hire trained cooks and bearers, but at this time, the household skills we practiced in our American homes bore little resemblance to those needed in East Pakistan.

In Hamza Mansion, the cook or bearer cleaned and prepared food while seated on the floor by a water faucet. The built-in cement hearths in each kitchen shared a common chimney, which facilitated the movement of huge cockroaches from floor to floor, enabling them to sample the food in every apartment. We used kerosene stoves for cooking, while most of the Bengalis preferred to use charcoal, which left every kitchen in the building black with soot.

The British and Australian missionaries in Chittagong did not screen their houses—perhaps they thought it a waste of money. The Barnards and Millers did not screen their houses either; so for our first two years in Chittagong, we also lived in unscreened apartments. Flies were a nuisance, but mosquitoes could be deadly. I fought a constant battle with malaria, almost from the beginning. When Edward Bomm, ABWE's treasurer, visited Chittagong, he listened to our stories about malaria, slept under a mosquito net, slapped at mosquitoes in broad daylight, and ordered us to screen our homes immediately. That simple act made a huge difference in our health and morale.

Missionaries must learn which foods must be carefully washed or disinfected and which must be avoided at all cost. As newcomers, we were slow learners; experience proved our best teacher. We often suffered from amoebic dysentery, but eventually, we learned to be more prudent about what we ate and drank. We also recognized the importance of not offending those who offered us food, often at great personal expense. When a Christian community eventually was established, Bengali believers zealously protected the missionaries' health by boiling the drinking water they served, using fewer chili peppers, and smiling understandingly when we had to refuse food "for my stomach's sake."

Although Chittagong was the second largest city in East Pakistan, we were not exempt from having to boil and filter our drinking water before it was safe. A visiting American sailor once asked, "How do you stay healthy here? I've had to use four times the usual amount of chlorine to purify the ship's water supply."

The apartment Juanita and I shared had city water, but the supply was limited. The landlord opened a valve and pumped water to a large tank on the roof of the apartment building, but he never knew exactly when the water would be turned on at the pumping station's main valve. When it was on, tenants had to turn on the kitchen and bathroom faucets and store enough water to last until the next time. If we happened to be away when the roof tank was filled, we might not get any water until later—or we might not get any at all! It depended on how full the roof tank was, and how much water our neighbors used. If someone wandered off and left a faucet open, he might drain the entire tank and no one would have water until the pumping station opened its main valve again.

Our greatest difficulty, of course, was our inability to communicate in the Bengali language. Mr. Barnard hired language teachers from among the young men who studied the Bible with him. None of them had taught language before, so it was up to us, as foreigners, to develop our own language curriculum. We had to learn simple household words, shopping terms, and the medical and religious terminology we needed for ministry. It was a slow process, equally frustrating to teachers and students alike, but, little by little, we did learn Bengali.

Juanita and I were frustrated at having been transplanted from an open, communicative society to what is called a "tea shop" society. Bengali men work away from home all day. They eventually go home to eat and sleep, but most men spend their leisure hours in neighborhood tea shops. They listen to the radio or watch TV and drink tea with their friends—all male, of course. In Muslim culture, women play only a limited role outside the home and have little knowledge of the world beyond their front doors. They cook, clean, carry water, and bear and raise children. When their husbands return from the fields, marketplace, or office, these women are not considered scintillating companions.

Our status as foreign women was much better than that of most Bengali women. Juanita and I, both nurses, were used to working in hospitals alongside male colleagues. Because we were trained in medicine, the national men assumed we must possess at least *some* intelligence. Later, when I worked at the ABWE hospital in Malumghat, I struggled to remain polite when Bengali husbands denigrated their wives. I fumed when a man said to me, "At least I can talk to you! I can't talk to my wife. She doesn't know anything." More than one man made that comment with his wife standing right next to him. Talk about women with low self-esteem!

There have been changes over the years. We used to see Muslim women wearing black *burkahs,* walking under big, black umbrellas. Gradually, the umbrellas disappeared and the all-encompassing *burkah* became less prominent.

When Juanita and I first lived in Chittagong in 1958, few motorized vehicles existed. There were many bicycle rickshaws, a few motorized baby taxis, an ancient taxicab or two, and a few privately owned cars and jeeps. According to the grapevine, the USAID (Agency for International Development) workers thought it scandalous that we missionaries used rickshaws to get around Chittagong. They thought that rickshaws were fine for Bengalis, but not for foreigners. It put the foreigner on display and was bad for our (translation: *their*) image. Besides, rickshaws were dangerous. I'm not sure what image we missionaries were meant to project, but using rickshaws was our only means of transportation, as well as the bane of our existence. Juanita and I had to travel around town, but we didn't know enough Bengali to give clear directions to a driver. Unless a Bengali speaker told the driver exactly where we were going and made sure our driver knew the way, we might end up anywhere in the city—and frequently did! Rickshaw pedaling is hard work, and our driver would inevitably take the first downhill route he could find.

After some months, Chittagong finally began to look a bit more familiar to us, but Juanita and I were often late or "no-shows" at scheduled events. The "rickshaw" adventures that our colleagues thought so hilarious served only to make us feel extremely foolish. However, the resulting frustration gave us an added incentive to learn the Bengali language as quickly as possible.

One day, during the time that I lived in a little bamboo house near the Tabernacle and Joyce Wingo was staying with me, the two of us ventured downtown to Chittagong's New Market to shop. Our dress was typical national costume: *shalwar* (baggy pants), *kamiz* (long tunic), and *dopatta* (long shawl). Our rickshaw sped along, bouncing over rough spots and potholes in the road. Joyce and I clutched the sides of our bench seat for dear life. Just as the driver reached my driveway, he hit the curb and we went flying, Joyce out her side of the rickshaw and I out mine. We were about to land in the dirt.

At that precise moment, a motorbike bearing two male riders *putt-putt-ed* out the driveway. Much to their astonishment, Joyce landed on one handlebar, and I landed on the other. It was a perfectly synchronized, superb acrobatic feat. Neither of us fell. We regained our balance, nodded politely at our knights in shining armor, and staggered back to my house, convulsed with laughter. The amazed looks on the men's faces were priceless. They must have wondered by what magic these white-faced foreigners dropped from the sky onto their handlebars.

• • •

How do missionaries befriend the nationals surrounding us? How can we possibly reach them with the gospel? We go overseas with education, ministry experience, and a great deal of idealism, then are appalled to discover that we need more than that to reach people of a different culture, language, and religion. How in the world can we do it? Where do we begin?

This problem was brought home to me in a new way when I moved to Hebron halfway through my first term in East Pakistan. Khoka Sen, a carpenter from Chittagong, came to help me in the medical work. He had been a Hindu before his conversion and knew the village mentality and the local dialect. My Bengali was still rudimentary, and I needed an interpreter to communicate with hill Bengalis and tribal people.

The villagers in the remote hill area near Hebron are primarily Buddhist, but probably had their religious origins in Hinduism centuries earlier. Muslims and animists also live in the area. A tiny Buddhist temple stands on the edge of Belchari village, not far from the Hebron clinic and the missionaries' houses.

Regular hours at the clinic and house calls in the neighborhood helped me get to know the villagers, but I had trouble figuring out how to reach people with no background in Christianity. The teenage girls were delighted when I told them Bible stories. "Oh," they would say, "the stories you tell sound just like the ones in our holy book!" The fact that God's Word is true made no impact on them at all. I asked God for wisdom in reaching out to these people. There was no way I could do it myself.

Early missionaries at Hebron faithfully tilled the hard soil of heathen hearts, planted the seed of God's Word, watered it with their tears, and deplored the slowness of its growth. We all had to learn that nothing we did would make that precious seed sprout. The Holy Spirit would accomplish His work in His own time. The seed *would* germinate and grow, and God *would* give an abundant harvest. Looking back on those difficult years, I can see that God kept His promise. He called out His people in that place and began to build His church.

Cultural, religious, and language barriers, and the loss of early missionaries to sickness and death—as well as Satan's determination to dislodge us from his territory—all played a part in making my first term as a missionary a grinding experience. That is exactly what it was: God was grinding and polishing me, making me a usable vessel in His hand. That first term laid the foundation for the years to come. As missionaries, we would see God work mightily as He built His church in the desperately needy country of East Pakistan.

four

We Rest on Thee

Death in a Third World country is vastly different from death in the United States, where we try to soften the blow with tastefully appointed funeral homes, beautiful flowers, soft music, dim lighting, expert embalming, and the comforting support of family and friends.

Shortly before we left for East Pakistan in 1958, ABWE's home office informed us that Winnifred Mary Barnard (called Mary), the vivacious, 14-year-old daughter of ABWE missionaries Victor and Winnifred Barnard, had died suddenly. We entered East Pakistan under that cloud. Her parents were coping well, but the death of a child always tears a huge hole in the fabric of a family. Mary was buried in the British cemetery outside Chittagong. This little cemetery, with its huge shade trees, crumbling walls, and old-fashioned headstones, had witnessed the burial of foreign travelers and missionaries for many years.

Victor and Winnifred spoke often about Mary, who had been the light of their lives. She first became ill while at boarding school in India. Miraculously, a surgeon was staying at the school, enjoying a holiday with his own children, Mary's fellow students. He operated on Mary for appendicitis, and she seemed to have a normal recovery. Winnifred noticed, however, that the next time Mary came home on holiday, she often complained of headaches. Winnifred was concerned, of course, but thought Mary was just getting over a difficult term at school and the lingering effects of surgery. Mary suddenly developed acute abdominal pain, however, and her condition grew steadily worse.

Victor frantically searched Chittagong for someone who could help. He found a female physician who treated Mary, but without success. Frightened by her deteriorating condition, her parents took Mary to the Railway Hospital. By the time her doctors suspected she had an intestinal obstruction (probably from scarring following the appendectomy), it was too late to save Mary's life. Strapped to a gurney while awaiting an X-ray, Mary quietly slipped away to her heavenly home.

Victor and Winnifred were devastated, but they had to remain strong for the rest of the family. Lauranne, their youngest girl, needed their comfort. Two older daughters were students at Baptist Bible College in Johnson City, New York. Victor and Winnifred tried to focus on the reason they lived in East Pakistan; they had come to bring the gospel to the Bengali people, and that mandate had not changed. New missionaries, arriving in just a few weeks, would need their counsel and assistance. While Victor and Winnifred grieved deeply for Mary, they continued on as best they could.

A year after I reached East Pakistan, Paul Miller, a gifted linguist and the father of four young children, came to Chittagong on business from the mission station Victor Barnard had named Hebron, which bordered the Chittagong Hill Tracts. Paul and his family had moved to Hebron with the Barnards so Paul could do Bible translation among the hill tribes. When he arrived in Chittagong, Paul was not feeling well and thought he might be coming down with malaria or dengue fever. Paul needed to see a doctor, but the Gurganuses and I didn't know where to find competent medical help. We had only lived in the country for a year and still felt like the newcomers we were.

In a tiny roadside medicine shop, I found injectable Thorazine, an anti-emetic that helped control Paul's nausea and vomiting. He was dehydrated and needed intravenous fluids, but the IV equipment I saw in the market was incredibly antiquated. Paul had also developed a one-sided weakness that worried me.

The hospitals in Chittagong did not possess adequate diagnostic or treatment facilities. "Paul," I said, "you're not getting any better here. I think we should send you to Holy Family Hospital in Dacca. They can diagnose your illness and give you the care you need." Gene Gurganus also urged Paul to let us get him to Dacca.

"Oh, no," Paul protested, "I really feel much better now that you've managed to control the vomiting. I'm sure I'll be fine in a few days." Seeing our concern, however, Paul finally conceded that our plan might be best.

I went to Major Oliver Omerod, a British friend who worked for the East Bengal Railway, and told him, "We think Paul needs to go to the hospital in Dacca as soon as possible. He's too sick to sit up in a railway car for 12 hours, and he still has some nausea. What would you suggest we do?"

Oliver replied, "I can arrange a private sleeper car for Paul so that he can lie down for the entire trip. It's the best way to get him to Dacca." Gene and I had cared for Paul non-stop since his arrival in Chittagong, and we were exhausted; so Joyce Wingo, a new missionary, and Oliver traveled with Paul to take care of his needs.

When Paul reached the hospital, it did not take the doctors long to suspect he was suffering from bulbar polio. Lab tests confirmed their diagnosis. The doctors and nurses did everything possible to save Paul's life. They even asked the American Air Force to fly in a respirator from West Pakistan. But less than 24 hours after his arrival in Dacca, Paul was dead. Oliver managed to phone Mr. and Mrs. Coffey, American friends in Chittagong, who brought the news to Gene, Beth, and me late on Sunday evening.

Paul's wife, Helen, and their four children were still at Hebron. I had sent a note by messenger to let Helen know Paul was ill. Now I had to send a second message to Hebron. Victor and Winnifred were still making frequent survey trips into the tribal areas surrounding Hebron at that time. Not knowing whether Helen was alone on the station, I wrote only that Paul's condition had worsened, and I asked Helen and the children to return to Chittagong with the messenger, if at all possible.

The night of Paul's death, Beth Gurganus and I sat up all night sewing a Christian flag to cover his casket. Paul's coffin would arrive from Dacca at the Chittagong train station early the following morning. We planned to hold his funeral at the building we used for church services and Bible studies. Gene and I didn't know how to arrange for Paul's burial, so we sought the advice of Mrs. Basanti Dass, our language teacher. Her husband was influential in the British Baptist church and would surely know the people who could help us make funeral arrangements. Mrs. Dass told Gene to contact the Anglican vicar, since the Anglicans maintained the English cemetery, and he graciously made sure a grave was opened and that everything was ready at the cemetery.

When Paul's casket arrived from Dacca, Major Omerod brought a message from the medical staff at Holy Family Hospital. They told us to bury Paul immediately. We must not open the casket, nor could we wait for his family to arrive from Hebron. Paul had died from a highly contagious disease, so we could only hold a graveside service. We covered the simple wooden coffin with the Christian flag and took it immediately to the cemetery. When we missionaries arrived, a number of people had already assembled. Representatives from the American Consul's office in Chittagong, American and European friends, and those from the local Christian community who had heard of Paul's death gathered for his funeral.

It was a bittersweet experience. Paul was in heaven. How could we wish him back? We rejoiced for him, but grieved for his family still traveling from Hebron. We missionaries were so few; how could we continue without Paul? We mourned the loss of our brother and colleague, as well as the great blow his death dealt to tribal translation. Now who would work with the tribal people?

Mrs. Dass traveled to the cemetery by rickshaw, carrying a bouquet of gardenias freshly picked from her front yard. It was the only floral tribute at Paul's funeral, and I remember its comfort as though it were yesterday. Joyce Wingo and I sang the beautiful hymn "We rest on Thee, our Shield and our Defender."

> We rest on Thee—our Shield and our Defender!
> Thine is the battle, Thine shall be the praise
> When passing through the gates of pearly splendor,
> Victors—we rest with Thee, through endless days.
>
> —*Edith G. Cherry*

We buried our brother, dried our tears, and prepared for the arrival of Helen and her children, Arnold, 11, Grace, 9, and 7-year-old twins Vernon and Sharon. God helped the family through the difficult days that followed. Later, He led them back to America and into other missionary service.

When Mary Barnard died, our good friend Major Omerod attended her funeral. Victor had witnessed to Oliver on many occasions, but observed that his words ran off Oliver like water off a duck's back. One day, Oliver told me about her funeral, saying, "As I stood by Mary's grave and listened to the preaching and music, I wished it would never end. I could not believe that a group of people mourning the loss of a child could be so full of joy. It was not like any funeral I had ever attended—it was so full of hope. Victor and Winnifred were absolutely certain they would see Mary again, and they could hardly wait for it to happen!"

What Oliver saw that day affected him far more than any of Victor's words. Not long after Mary's funeral, Oliver made a personal commitment to Christ. With Paul Miller's burial, he witnessed another Christian funeral, but this time Oliver stood with the believers: grieving, yet rejoicing in the fact that Paul was in heaven, and knowing he would see him again.

Is death in a heathen land stark? Yes, appallingly so. Yet even in death, Christ can give peace, joy, and the glorious hope of a coming resurrection. We can trust the One who lifts our loved one in His arms, carries him to heaven, and whispers the promise that we *shall indeed* meet in heaven and never have to say good-bye again.

five

Introduction to Third World Medicine

Medical practice in the developing world can be a shock, especially when one is coming straight from a well-equipped American hospital, and my introduction to hospitals and midwives in Chittagong was downright scary. When ABWE later established a hospital at Malumghat, we made strict rules about sanitation and nursing care. But, at this time, Memorial Christian Hospital was still eight years in the future.

Winnifred Barnard, who enjoyed a warm relationship with her neighbors, gave me my first glimpse of medicine in Bangladesh. She and Victor rented an apartment on the second floor of a building situated in one of the oldest areas of Chittagong. Victor used the first floor as a preaching hall and called it the Tabernacle. Most of Winnifred's neighbors were Hindus. If they became ill, they went to a local doctor or homeopathic practitioner. Practically all babies were born at home with the help of a midwife. Most Bengalis never saw the inside of a hospital unless they were desperately ill or badly injured. The hospitals in Chittagong at that time had the same reputation European hospitals had in the 1800s, before the discovery of germs and sterilization. Bengalis thought of hospitals as places to go only when there was no hope of recovery.

One day Winnifred told me, "I'm going to a neighbor's house. She's about to give birth, and I thought you might like to observe the delivery. I know they won't mind if you come. I'm sure we'll find the house full of female relatives." We walked across the courtyard to a tiny bamboo house where Winnifred introduced me to the expectant mother and the female relatives attending her. "Miss Brownell is a nurse from America," she said. "I thought she'd be interested in watching the midwife deliver the baby." I was just an observer, so I kept my hands behind my back and bit my tongue to keep quiet.

Many houses in Chittagong were bamboo huts with mud floors. Some had only one room, where the family lived in close proximity 24 hours a day. Most had a separate place for cooking, either a small room in the hut or a bamboo shack behind the house. In this household, the cooking shack was a small, walled-off area behind the main room. The expectant mother lay on the mud floor of this room with a few burlap sacks under her. Many Bengalis sleep on the floor anyhow, so this was not unusual. The women would throw away the burlap sacks after the delivery and could easily clean the mud floor with the traditional mixture of mud and cow manure. I was shocked by what appeared to be a total disregard for cleanliness, but the Bengali women were obviously comfortable with the arrangements.

The native midwife arrived and prepared for the delivery. Much to my dismay, she dropped her scissors on the mud floor. She had wrapped a bit of string around them so she could tie off the umbilical cord. She calmly picked up her scissors, dusted them off with her hand, and set them on the table. Preparations for the delivery did not include boiling water, and the midwife had no rubbing alcohol or disinfectant with which to wipe her scissors. She didn't wash her hands, either. Despite the lack of sterile technique, she delivered a beautiful, healthy boy and presented him to his delighted mother. The midwife obviously knew her job; I'm sure that she delivered many babies in the community.

Later I learned the childbirth statistics in East Pakistan at that time. Many mothers died a few days after a perfectly normal delivery. There were good reasons for this, although reading about it made me feel as though I had stepped back into the Dark Ages. Shortly after delivery, new mothers took a ritual bath, usually in a nearby pond. People use these neighborhood ponds for everything imaginable: washing their cows, bathing, brushing their teeth, washing dishes, laundering clothes, filling the tea kettle, and any other job that calls for water. Naturally, the ponds were highly contaminated, and the vulnerable new mother often succumbed to an overwhelming infection. I was amazed that so many mothers and babies survived the trauma of an unclean delivery and the rituals that followed.

• • •

When ABWE missionary Joyce Wingo arrived in Chittagong for language study, she shared my small bamboo house next to the Tabernacle. We visited Hebron together, and she fell in love with the tribal people. She had a burden for translation work and hoped to begin translating the Bible into their language, called Tripura. Joyce and I decided to move to Hebron, where she would do Bible translation and I would do medical work.

Because of this, our houseboy, Barik, had already moved across town to work for Juanita Canfield and Miriam Morin, who were also missionaries. Barik's brother, Jabbor, came to work for Joyce and me because he planned to move to Hebron with us. Before Joyce and I moved from Chittagong, however, Barik had a serious accident. He was riding his bike through town at dusk when a military jeep struck him and knocked him off his bicycle. The soldiers picked him up and took him to General Hospital. Barik had five broken ribs and a serious head injury.

Juanita and I split Barik's nursing care between us. I stayed with him at night, and Juanita stayed at the hospital during the day. Aziz, one of our language teachers, shared the shift with me that first night. As we sat listening to Barik's labored breathing, we were sure he wouldn't last through the night. I don't know what was most unnerving about that dreadful night: the numbing fear of losing Barik, my inability to help him, or the huge rats that roamed the ward. The night nurse and orderly were gracious, but there was not much they could do for Barik. After all, he was unconscious, and they, too, were sure he would die.

I watched with horror as the night nurse filled a large syringe with penicillin. She went from bed to bed, giving each patient his share of the medicine, never changing needles or swabbing injection sites.

One patient on the ward called out every time I walked past his bed. "Nurse," I said, "the man that's groaning seems to be in terrible distress. Can't you give him something to relieve his pain?"

She shrugged and said, "He's going to die. Besides, I have nothing to give him. The doctor didn't leave an order for pain medication."

Barik lived through four agonizing days before succumbing to pneumonia. It was hard to see him die, but even harder to watch him struggle for breath in such wretched surroundings.

• • •

One afternoon I was awakened from my siesta by Gene Gurganus, who was standing outside the door calling my name. "Mary Lou, there's a little girl here who needs help," he said. "You'd better come right away!"

I nodded sleepily, washed my face and ran a comb through my hair, then walked next door to the Tabernacle, where I looked with disbelief at the disfigured child standing in front of me. "What happened to her?" I asked, then listened as her uncle explained. Five days earlier, the child, named Mathaiu, had fallen from the porch of her family's home after dark. Since Moghs build their houses on stilts, she fell nearly eight feet to the ground, landing on the sharp edge of a machete someone had used to prepare the evening meal. The knife cut through the bony part of her nose, leaving a deep gash and an open wound nearly three inches long.

Mathaiu's village was near Hebron, so the girl's father and uncle had taken her first to the mission station there for medical help. However, the missionaries at Hebron knew they could not help her, so they sent her to us. Now little Mathaiu stood silently in the Tabernacle in Chittagong, awaiting our verdict.

Someone had covered her wound with a thin strip of absorbent cotton, which was now stuck in place with dried blood. I was afraid to remove the dressing, wondering what I would do if the gash started bleeding again.

After the disastrous experience with Barik in the local hospital, I decided there had to be a better option. "Gene," I said, "we can't take Mathaiu there. If we do, she'll die." We had little knowledge of reputable clinics or trustworthy doctors. "There's an Irish Catholic priest in Feringhee Bazar," I remembered. "I met him one day when I visited his school. He runs a small clinic and treats his own parishioners. Do you suppose he'd be willing to help?"

Gene thought for a moment. "I honestly don't know anywhere else we can take her," he said. "At least the priest can give us advice about treatment."

We bundled Mathaiu, her father, and uncle into Gene's jeep and drove to the clinic. The priest, who received us graciously, determined that we must expose the wound to assess Mathaiu's condition. He brought me a bowl of water and instructed, "Here, you soak the dressing while I go and say a little prayer." I soaked the area, then cautiously removed the dressing under the priest's watchful eye. It was a slow, painful process, but Mathaiu never even whimpered. There was no bleeding, but the wound was badly infected.

"Look," the priest said, "we can't take care of this here. Why don't you send her to Holy Family Hospital in Dacca? They have a competent plastic surgeon on staff, and they'll take good care of her." Gene and I talked with Mathaiu's father, emphasizing that this was the girl's only chance for survival.

That night we sent Mathaiu off to Dacca with her father, her uncle, and Benu Pundit, one of the language teachers. Mathaiu and her relatives had never ventured to Dacca before and were frightened. I'm sure they never would have gone to the hospital if we had not sent Benu to accompany them.

Anxious days of uncertainty followed. Mathaiu had lost so much blood that she needed transfusions before the surgeon could operate. She survived the operation, but her condition was precarious. Several weeks passed before Mathaiu was strong enough to return to Chittagong. Her father and uncle had returned to their Mogh village, so Benu brought Mathaiu to us to see if she needed further treatment.

It seemed like a miracle to see her alive and well. The wound had healed completely, but the little girl's face was badly scarred. Thank God, the knife had missed her eyes. The scar didn't seem to bother Mathaiu, and her big, happy smile made the scar less noticeable. She knew she was finally going home and almost danced with excitement at the thought.

There was nothing further that could be done medically for Mathaiu, so Joyce and I offered to take her back to her family. We caught the night train from Chittagong to Dohazari, then made the long bus ride to the Matamahari River. A long dugout canoe with pointed ends, known as a country boat, took us to Manikpur, a large Mogh village, where the villagers were astonished to see Mathaiu. Because she had been gone so long, they were sure she had died. Now here she was: alive, well, and happy.

We stayed overnight at Manikpur while the village headman arranged for us to be escorted to Mathaiu's village. The next morning, we walked miles through dense jungle, trudged up and down steep hills, forded shallow rivers, and slipped and slid in thick mud. Joyce and I discovered that we were bleeding from several areas on our legs and feet—our first introduction to leeches. The Mogh headman touched the glowing tip of his cigar to each leech, causing it to drop off. "You have to do that," he explained. "If they fall off, the bleeding will stop. But if you pull at them, the wound will continue to bleed for a long time."

As we approached her village, Mathaiu was so excited she started to run, but Joyce and I were apprehensive about her reception. Would her family accept her—scarred face and all? We need not have worried. The villagers greeted Mathaiu with delight, and her mother received her daughter with open arms and tears of joy.

As chatting neighbors filled Mathaiu's house, Joyce and I rested. We ate a bountiful meal, prepared by Mathaiu's mother, before our long walk back to our country boat. After we said our goodbyes and began walking down the long hill leading away from the village, we heard a little voice calling, "Hi!" We turned to see Mathaiu waving and blowing kisses. It was a happy ending to a story that might have ended in tragedy.

• • •

When Jay and Eleanor Walsh and their three young children arrived in Chittagong in 1959, Eleanor was expecting her fourth child. Because of our experiences with hospitals in East Pakistan, we thought it would be unwise for her to have the baby in Dacca. The Walsh family flew to West Pakistan to await the baby's arrival. They took a language teacher with them so they could study Bengali while they waited. While the Walshes were in West Pakistan, the whole ABWE picture in East Pakistan changed. The Barnards were preparing for furlough, and Helen Miller was getting ready to take her children back to the U.S. after Paul's death. Gene Gurganus had sent Beth, Lydia, and baby Martha home for medical care, and he had moved to Hebron temporarily so that

Joyce and I could remain there with the culturally required male protection. After baby Phillip's birth, Jay came to Hebron so that Gene could orient him to the work on the station. Gene then left to join Beth and their children in North Carolina, while Jay retrieved his family from West Pakistan.

My first memory of Eleanor Walsh at Hebron is that of watching her climb the muddy riverbank with baby Phil tucked securely under one arm. All four Walsh children, Doug, Linda, Debbie, and even little Phillip, took to new experiences like ducklings take to water. Even though Hebron was extremely isolated, Jay and El managed to care for their family and establish a home while studying the language and visiting Bengali families and tribal people. Theirs was an incredibly difficult transition, but they did it with grace and courage. They, like the other early missionaries at Hebron, laid a strong foundation for the Bengali and tribal ministries which would expand in years to come.

When Eleanor learned she was expecting twins, she and Jay once again went to West Pakistan so the babies could be born at the Christian Hospital in Lahore. Meanwhile, the four Walsh children and I, along with their big German shepherd, shared an apartment in Chittagong. We eagerly awaited news of the delivery, and we finally received word in November that El had given birth to twin girls. The Walsh kids entertained themselves thinking up fanciful names for their new sisters, like Jello and Jelly, which sent them off into fits of giggles. We were very happy when Jay and El arrived in Chittagong with the babies named Sheryl Ann and Shelley Lou. The twins were beautiful babies—small, but perfectly healthy.

In 1962, near the end of my first term, the Walshes and I, along with newly arrived ABWE missionaries Lynn Silvernale and Donna Ahlgrim, were anticipating the arrival of our first medical doctor, Viggo Olsen. The Walshes had relocated to Chittagong after the twins' birth because there was a great deal of administrative work there that only Jay could do. I had moved in with Jay and El to help look after the kids, as well as help prepare for the new missionaries.

Dr. Viggo (Vic) Olsen, his wife, Joan, and their four young children, Wendy, Mark, Lynn, and Nancy, arrived in East Pakistan in January of that year. The entire Olsen family had recently spent time in England, where Vic, an experienced surgeon, studied tropical medicine. His medical expertise would soon face its first major test in East Pakistan.

Shortly after the Olsen's arrival, Sheryl Walsh, the smallest of the three-month-old twins, became ill with diarrhea. In the tropics, diarrhea is an insidious enemy. It can lead quickly to dehydration, which, if untreated, results in circulatory collapse and sudden death.

Vic kept a close eye on her, and she seemed to be slowly improving. But El Walsh and I woke early one morning to discover that she was in distress. When El asked Vic to check on Sheryl, he took one look and knew that only immediate action would save her life. Our first choice was to take her by car to Chandraghona, a Baptist Mission Hospital about forty miles away. But at the last minute, as we stood by the car, Vic said, "We've got to find help fast. It will take us at least an hour to get to Chandraghona. She won't last that long. We'll have to take her to the closest hospital."

Rushing into the emergency room of nearby Medical College Hospital, Vic asked for intravenous equipment. There was no sterile equipment, but the staff put what he requested into a small sterilizer. El Walsh, herself a nurse, walked into the room a few minutes later and saw with horror that the equipment was indeed in the sterilizer and steam was rising, but no one had put down the cover—the sterilizer was wide open.

Vic knew we were running out of time. He set up the IV and took the needle in his hand while I held the IV bottle in one hand, steadying Sheryl on the examining table with my other hand. Starting intravenous fluid on a tiny baby is difficult at best, but Sheryl was barely breathing. "Just keep your hand on her while I try to find a vein I can use," Vic said. "Her veins have collapsed and she's going into circulatory failure." We prayed silently for God's help and intervention. Jay and El retreated to their car, where they entrusted Sheryl to the hands of a loving heavenly Father.

While Vic worked desperately to start the IV, a group of Bengali doctors gathered around the table. They watched with interest as Vic probed Sheryl's tiny veins. I'm sure she looked half dead to them, because she was unconscious and blue halfway up her arms. Her life was fast slipping away. One of the onlookers asked, "Doctor, what are you trying to do?"

As he worked, Vic explained patiently, "This baby is so dehydrated that her circulation is failing. If we don't give her fluids immediately, she will die." Vic quietly continued probing while the doctors thought this over.

Finally, one doctor expressed the opinion of all. "You know, Doctor," he said, "we wouldn't do that in this country. If we had a baby in that condition, we'd just let her die."

His statement was unnecessary; Vic and I had already figured that out. The doctors acted as though we were crazy to expend so much energy on a dying baby. Finally, the large needle slipped into a vein in Sheryl's groin, allowing her to quickly get the fluids she needed. Vic cut adhesive tape and secured the needle firmly in place.

"Will she make it?" I breathed, almost afraid to ask.

Vic glanced at me sideways while he continued taping down the tubing. "You know the IV equipment wasn't sterile," he said. I nodded. "Sheryl has a chance," he said, "if she can overcome the infection from that contaminated needle."

The hospital administrator told us he couldn't admit Sheryl, but Chittagong General Hospital, halfway across town, would provide the facilities needed for her care. I put her on a pillow, picked her up—IV tubing, needle, and all—and carried her to the car. She was admitted to a private room in the downtown hospital. She looked so tiny lying on the bed, pale and wan, her big blue eyes wide open. If Sheryl was to survive, nurse Lynn Silvernale and I would have to care for her round-the-clock.

Lynn and I rotated eight-hour shifts for the next five days. Sheryl didn't whimper or cry; she just lay on the bed, her eyes following us as we moved around the room. She had a huge abscess in her groin from the contaminated equipment. Vic lanced the abscess and gave her antibiotics, and we all prayed earnestly for her. God graciously touched that little body and healed Sheryl. It was a joyful day when Jay and El brought her home from the hospital.

How thankful we were for Vic's presence when Sheryl became desperately ill. We still had two wonderful babies, and for that we would always be grateful. It was a happy ending to my traumatic introduction to Third World medicine.

six

Consenting to Their Death

Khoka was a faithful Bengali helper from the early days of ABWE's ministry in East Pakistan. He worked in a furniture shop near the Barnards' home in Chittagong. Victor Barnard purchased his household furniture from the shop where Khoka worked and got to know him quite well. When Khoka visited the Barnard home to give the furniture a final coat of polish, Victor used the opportunity to talk to him about Christ. Khoka seemed interested in Christianity, but he was a Hindu. Since his employer was Muslim, he had to be very circumspect. If his employer knew Khoka was studying Christianity or if his association with Christian foreigners was made too obvious, Khoka might lose his job. Then who would care for his wife and children, who lived in a village outside Chittagong? Khoka eventually trusted Christ, but it would be several years before I learned the circumstances that brought him to faith.

When I moved to Hebron in 1960, halfway through my first term, Khoka was by then a Christian, and willingly came along to help in the dispensary. He could not bring his wife and children with him because someone had to occupy the family home so it would not be looted or claimed by squatters. Khoka screened patients, handed out medicines under my supervision, and accompanied me on sick calls to the villages, since it was culturally improper for me to venture out in public alone. Whenever I needed to send a messenger to Chittagong, Khoka went, traveling the more than eighty miles by boat and bus. If he left at night and made good connections, he could reach Chittagong by the next afternoon. Khoka served as my companion and protector when I had to travel to Chittagong. I still struggled with the intricacies of the Bengali language, so he often acted as my interpreter. Khoka also spoke the dialect used in the area around Hebron, which helped me tremendously.

After he began growing spiritually, Khoka sometimes was asked to preach in the Bengali church services. One afternoon, several years after he was saved, I was stunned by a sermon in which he related an incident that occurred just a few weeks after my arrival in East Pakistan. Its impact had been devastating then, and his review brought memories flooding back. What Khoka said was even more shocking. He graphically described what had happened, and then said, "And I was consenting to their death."

Khoka was relating the details of an attack on Victor, Winnifred, and Lauranne Barnard; David Coffey; Gene Gurganus; Dr. Pierce Samuels, a missionary serving in a remote tribal area; Juanita Canfield; and me. A few weeks after I first arrived in Chittagong, the missionaries met at the Tabernacle for the Friday afternoon service. Because Friday is the Muslim holy day, Muslim men thronged the streets on their way to the local mosque (Muslim temple), just a short walk down the block, for their special weekly service. The missionaries gathered on the upstairs verandah of Victor and Winnifred Barnard's house, and Victor turned on the loud speaker. We sang some Bengali hymns, and Juanita and I sang a duet in English. Then Victor began to preach. The singing and preaching drew a large group of men to the courtyard below us. The men watched Victor closely and listened intently to his words.

Without warning, a stone flew through the air, shattering a window, and suddenly our quiet, intent congregation turned into an angry, screaming, stone-throwing mob. We hastily retreated inside, closing the wooden shutters that covered the windows. The men outside picked up bricks and large stones, hurling them at the building. I will always remember the sickening thud of bricks hitting concrete and wood with great force.

We sat in a circle and prayed, asking God to deliver us if that was His will. Just that morning I had read the words "pray that we may be delivered from unreasonable and wicked men: for all men have not faith" (2 Thessalonians 3:2). The verse had never caught my attention before, but it was certainly appropriate at that particular moment.

David Coffey, a friend of 14-year-old Lauranne Barnard, was spending the day with the Barnard family. During a lull in the riot, David's father, who worked for USAID, appeared at the perimeter of the mob and somehow received permission to retrieve his son from the building. He called loudly, "David, come to me," and David fled to the safety of his father's arms.

Inside, we were painfully aware that only two flimsy doors of the old Tabernacle building stood between our little group and that angry, roaring mob. Only God could keep them outside the building. As the riot escalated, Victor Barnard wanted to go outside, confront the ringleaders, and ask for deliverance. All of us, especially Gene and Pierce, objected loudly. We thought that any contact with missionaries—particularly Victor—might inflame the mob to violence. We were afraid that the mob would kill him, and insisted he remain quietly hidden from sight. He finally called out a side window to a neighbor, asking him to summon the police. But most of the neighbors were Hindus, and it seemed a vain hope that any of them would brave the Muslim mob to reach a telephone.

At one point, several of the mob leaders left the courtyard. We could hear them shouting complaints against us on the busy street corner, trying to enlist others to join their cause, and we knew they could storm the building at any moment. There was no way out of the building that would not expose us to more danger. We could do nothing but pray, committing ourselves to the mercy of God.

Then a huge flatbed truck roared into the courtyard, scattering the mob in every direction. Policemen jumped off the truck and banged loudly on the outside door, and Victor ran downstairs to open it. We learned that a young Hindu neighbor, risking his life, had run through a back alley to phone the police. God had, indeed, delivered us from the hands of unreasonable and wicked men.

We came downstairs, our faces wreathed in smiles, amazed and overjoyed at God's miraculous intervention. The police were shocked to discover women in the building. They couldn't believe the men had been so violent, knowing we were on the second floor. The first person I saw was Khoka. He stood near Victor, ashen-faced. God had saved us from certain death while he stood and watched.

A few days after this incident Khoka had appeared in Victor's office, saying that he had to accept Jesus Christ as Savior. He knew, from long experience, the futility of pagan worship. While Khoka had worshipped idols all his life, he confessed to Victor that Hinduism had been a source of disillusionment to him for many years. From childhood, Khoka had heard of Christ and His sacrificial death for sins. Until the riot, however, Khoka had not understood the reality of God's incredible power. The seed planted in his heart by Victor's witness sprang to life. Now he had seen God's power and wanted what the Christians had. "How could they be so unafraid of death?" he asked Victor. "How could they come downstairs smiling after they almost died?" If Christ could do that for a person, Khoka had to have Christ. Victor led Khoka to Christ right there in his office.

The day I heard Khoka preach, he was talking about the apostle Paul. He reminded us that those who stoned Stephen laid their coats at the feet of Saul, who consented to Stephen's death. As a self-righteous Jew, Saul probably felt that Stephen got exactly what he deserved. Khoka didn't throw stones, but when we were attacked, he was right there with the stone-throwing mob outside the Tabernacle. What difference did it make to him whether we lived or died? Khoka certainly had no intention of defending us in the middle of *that* mob!

Khoka pointed out that it was probably Stephen's victorious death that burned itself into Saul's mind and prepared him to accept Jesus Christ as his Lord and Savior. Khoka knew just how Saul felt! There was one important difference in the two stories, however. Stephen died at the hands of an angry mob; we missionaries were privileged to live. It was not our *deaths* that brought Khoka to Christ, but the fact that God protected us and spared our lives from mortal danger.

seven

Faith Comes by Hearing

Widespread illiteracy was one of the most difficult problems I faced in my early years in East Pakistan. As a bibliophile who reads everything in sight, I find it hard to fathom the fact that millions of people in the world can't pick up a book and read it with keen enjoyment. God's Word says, "So then faith cometh by hearing, and hearing by the word of God" (Romans 10:17). One of the delights of God's Word is reading it over and over until the words imprint themselves on our minds, leading us to know and do God's will.

Teaching an illiterate person about God involves repeating the lesson many times, patiently explaining the concept. Bible verses must be taught by rote; teacher and pupil recite the verse again and again until the student commits it to memory. Bengalis have incredible memories. Many of them grow up illiterate and must memorize a great many facts in order to survive. But just because something is committed to memory does not mean that the concept has been understood.

I faced this fact in Chittagong when I taught illiterate people for the first time. When missionary Reid Minich arrived in Chittagong in 1963, Monindro, a Bengali man, cleaned Reid's house and did his laundry and cooking. Reid witnessed often to Monindro and eventually he accepted Christ as his Savior.

Monindro then faced a major problem. He said to Reid, "If I tell my wife she needs to accept Christ, she'll say, 'Fine. If that's what you want, that's what I'll do.' I don't want her to believe just because I tell her she needs to. I want her to become a believer

Paul and Helen Miller with children Arnold, Grace, Vernon, and Sharon.

Hebron pioneers Jay and Eleanor Walsh.

Shabi teaching in the village.

Prova with one of her beautiful grandsons.

Gupi John, Chobi, Mary Lou, Shabi, and Becky Davey.

Medical personnel at Memorial Christian Hospital.

Khoka baptizes a new believer.

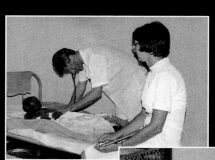

Dr. Donn Ketcham with a new baby.

Dr. Joe DeCook and Dorothy Adams examine a young patient.

Bob Adolph with two lab technicians in training.

Shabi ministering at Heart House.

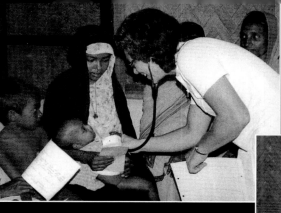

Becky Davey examines patients in the outpatient department.

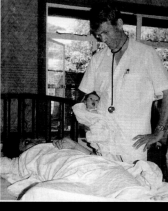

Dr. Joe DeCook with a mother and her new baby.

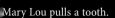

Mary Lou pulls a tooth.

Mrs. Dhar with her three youngest children on the day of her husband's funeral.

Nurse Jean Weld with a new mother.

Older MKs at Malumghat, in costume for the Bicentennial concert.

Cast of *You're A Good Man, Charlie Brown*. Malumghat MKs: (front row, left to right) Amy DeCook, Ricky Adolph, Diane Walsh, Kathy Stagg, Kristen Stagg, Tim Golin (Pigpen), Susie Beals; (back row, left to right) Dave DeCook, Dan DeCook, Steve DeCook, David Ketcham, Dan Golin, Kim Beals, Steve Adolph, and Karen Stagg.

The Malumghat MK school choir.

Mary Lou, Prova, and Jimmie Nusca.

Mary Lou holds one of Prova's boys.

because she understands she's a sinner and accepts Christ's death as payment for her sins. And then there's Mother," he added. "What do I do about her?"

Reid asked Monindro why he didn't just explain the gospel to her. Monindro said, "You don't understand. In my country, sons don't tell their mothers anything! Mothers know everything. It isn't proper for me to tell her about my new faith. It would only make her angry. Because she lives in my house I *can* tell her she can't worship idols any more, but that's all. I can't tell her about Christ, and I can't teach her. What am I going to do?"

Reid responded, "Monindro, I believe God can bring your whole family to Christ. He wants your wife and mother to believe on Jesus Christ and be saved. Do you think they would let one of the missionary ladies teach them?"

Monindro smiled. "Oh, yes," he said. "I'm sure if they hear the gospel from one of the ladies, they'll want to receive Christ. That's a wonderful idea! Please find someone to teach them."

Since I was living in Chittagong at the time, Reid asked me if I would teach Monindro's wife and mother. Monindro lived on a large plot of ground he inherited from his father. He owned a bamboo house where he, his wife, mother, and young nephew lived. On two sides of the large courtyard, Monindro had built small bamboo houses that he rented out to provide a steady income for his family.

Before he found Christ, Monindro was a Hindu, and the tenants surrounding his house also were Hindus. The first time I visited Monindro's home I wondered about his neighbors. How would they react, living next door to a converted Hindu? Would Monindro's family face persecution? What would the neighbors think when the women studied the Christian faith? Bamboo houses offer little privacy; arguments, wild grief or joy, singing lessons, religious training—the neighbors overhear it all.

Monindro's mother, often called Old Ma, and his wife, Renu, listened with interest as I taught them who Christ was and what He had done for them. I showed them from the Bible how we displease God when we worship idols instead of the true God.

It was uphill work. Illiterate people can seem unresponsive, possibly because they are not used to absorbing new material. They can't read for themselves; they can only listen. Perhaps they also have a hard time deciding what kind of response the teacher expects. I wasn't sure I was getting through to them until one day Old Ma began to talk to me. What she said showed me clearly that the Holy Spirit was working in her heart.

"Teacher," she began, "I really do want to worship the true God. Monindro told me I couldn't worship idols anymore. Believe me, Teacher, I don't. But I have such a hard problem that I don't know what to do. I really need your help." This was an incredibly long speech for the old woman.

"Please," I urged, "tell me your problem, and I'll do my best to help you." She walked to one side of the room and opened a bamboo door I hadn't noticed before. Inside was an idol shelf with framed pictures of Hindu deities. I thought, What is her problem? And why are the idols still here if she doesn't worship them? Please, Lord, help me understand what she's talking about.

Monindro's mother continued, "Teacher, these god pictures belonged to my mother and to her mother before her. You say that if I want to worship God, I must destroy my idols. But tell me, Teacher, how can I destroy these pictures that have been in my family for so many years?"

Comprehension struck me like a bolt of lightning: These aren't her idols anymore. These are her family antiques. She doesn't want to throw away her inherited family treasures!

"Old Ma," I said, "you can't worship the true God while you still have an idol shelf in the house. And you can't give your idols to someone else to keep either. You have to destroy them if you want God to bless your life and family." I knew she had to make the decision herself. I prayed with her, asking God to help her take the idols out of her life and destroy them. Nothing less would solve her problem.

A few days later I met Monindro's nephew, Shudhir, in the market, and he stopped to talk for a minute. He said, "I had so much fun when Old Ma carried her holy pictures out into the courtyard and set fire to them. She let me stomp on the frames and break them up. Then she threw them on the fire, too. The neighbors were angry and afraid, and they are sure the gods will punish Old Ma for being disrespectful. But she's not afraid. She knows God will take care of her."

And He did. The fearlessness of her mother-in-law helped bring Renu to acceptance of Christ as her personal Savior. When Old Ma became ill and the neighbors prophesied her imminent death, God healed her and raised her up overnight. When neighbors refused to let Monindro's family use the local tube well because they were Christians, God intervened to help the family. The local union council chairman (mayor), neither a Christian nor a Hindu, made it clear that the neighbors must not interfere with Monindro's family in any way. As chairman of Monindro's district, he was responsible for the family's protection, and he took his responsibility seriously.

Monindro had decided to postpone his baptism until his wife and mother were ready to be baptized, too. When they finally decided to be baptized, I told Reid, "I still can't imagine Renu or Old Ma giving a public testimony. Their pre-baptismal interview before the deacons may be a fiasco!"

As I sat and listened to Renu's testimony of personal faith in Christ, however, I was overwhelmed and could only praise God for His grace. Renu said quietly, "When my husband accepted Christ, I was afraid of what would happen. I knew that Christians often face persecution, and we live in a Hindu community. Then I saw how God took care of us, even when we were in danger. When I learned about God and all He has done for me, how He sent His own dear Son to the cross to save me, I decided to follow Him. I'm thankful for those who came to tell us about Jesus Christ, and I want to be baptized and become part of the church."

When Old Ma told clearly how she had come to faith in Christ, I could hardly contain my joy. "I want you to know that I was not happy when my son decided to change his religion," she began. "Our family has worshipped together as Hindus for as long as I can remember. Why should that change because my son heard something new? Then Teacher showed me that worshipping idols makes the true God sad because He wants us to worship Him with all our heart. I felt sorry that I was making the true God sad because I worshipped idols. I listened to Teacher for many weeks before I finally decided that I wanted to worship the true God who loved me enough to send His Son to take away my sins. I destroyed my idols because I want God to bless our family. Now I'm happy that my son, his wife, and I can be baptized at the same time. We're ready for heaven now, and that makes me happy, too."

Listening to these testimonies, I knew beyond a shadow of a doubt that this could not have happened without God's personal intervention. *He* opened their spiritual ears; *He* made His Word clear and plain; *He* brought Monindro, Renu, and Old Ma to the point of total commitment to Christ. Faith comes by hearing (even when we cannot read), but enlightenment and understanding come only through the amazing work of the Holy Spirit.

eight

Overnight on a Salt Boat

Life on the mission field often is filled with mundane routine. The ordinary tasks of living take a lot more time in a developing nation than they do in the United States. Even with household helpers, major decisions, minor crises, and countless frustrations take their toll on one's good humor. And there are also adventures—the kind you must go halfway around the world to experience.

While I lived at Hebron during my first term, someone had to make the trip to Chittagong once a month to withdraw money from the bank, buy supplies at the market, and take care of the business we couldn't handle in our remote area. When Jay and Eleanor Walsh lived at Hebron, Jay and I usually traded this duty. That way, the same person did not have to leave Hebron every month. The trip also provided an opportunity to visit friends, shop, eat in a restaurant, and experience bustling city life.

The trip involved a bus ride of sixty miles from Cheringha to Chittagong. But first, we had to get from Hebron to Cheringha, a distance of fifteen to twenty miles, and the only way to do that was by small riverboat. This was a quiet, relaxing boat ride, offering time to sleep, read, or watch the jungle slip by. Going upriver or downriver meant spending a night in the small boat or at a Mogh village along the way. *Majhis* (boatmen) rowed or poled the boat, depending on the river's depth, which varied throughout the year, since water recedes rapidly once the heavy monsoon rains stop. In summer, the trip was hot and exhausting, even though a woven bamboo *pong* (canopy) covers each boat to keep the sun and rain off of passengers and cargo.

One day when I was in Chittagong, getting ready to return to Hebron after finishing all my errands, Gene Gurganus stopped by the Tabernacle to tell me about an amazing new motorboat he wanted to try out. He planned to return to Hebron the following day, using the new boat. Grinning, Gene said, "If you're finished with everything in town, how about a fast trip back to Hebron? Two Bengali friends are going along to help, but there's plenty of room for you. It should only take us a few hours to get to Lama Bazar; we can walk the two miles to Hebron from there. Everyone says it's a quick trip if you have a good speedboat." Gene planned to go out the mouth of the Kharnafuli River in Chittagong and meet up with the Matamahari River not far from the port town of Cox's Bazar. It sounded good to me and, since I had finished my work in Chittagong, I took Gene up on his offer.

Gene arrived before dawn the next morning. Because it was winter, the morning air was crisp and cool, promising a beautiful day for travel. We rode a rickshaw to the boat landing. When we got into our powerboat, stars still danced in the sky. What fun to travel in a fast boat instead of wasting the entire day in a train and bus!

But wait a minute. Why were all the riverboats coming toward us instead of heading toward the mouth of the river? Whoa! Somebody forgot to check the tide chart, and we were traveling against the tide. The Bengali boatman hired for this particular stretch of river was seated at the front of the boat. He seemed totally unconcerned as boats whizzed by on both sides. Until it was light enough to see oncoming boats, I spent my time yelling, "Boatman, show your light!" He had a flashlight. Why didn't the man use it?

We finally arrived at the mouth of the Kharnafuli River and left our less-than-helpful guide behind. Now we were on our own. We assumed that someone in our boat knew how to reach the Matamahari River. We went on—and on—and on. Where in the world were we? Did anyone know? Had we lost the Matamahari River completely?

We came at last to a totally blocked channel, full of silt and prepared for dredging. How would we get Gene's boat to the next channel? Was it even possible? I still don't believe what happened next. A huge flatbed truck came roaring across the dry fields, trailing a cloud of dust. Coolies swarmed off the truck, lifted Gene's boat onto the flatbed, and carted it to the next open channel. Visions of getting to "our" river receded into the background. The big question now was: Would we ever get home?

Traveling such a long distance had depleted our supply of gasoline. We had to find a village with a supply of gas *and* the willingness to sell us this precious commodity. Several missing elements made the trip less than ideal. Gas for the boat would be helpful; food would be appreciated; toilet facilities were becoming an absolute necessity.

A kind man finally sold us gasoline; a watermelon quenched our thirst; accessible outhouses along the river provided primitive restrooms. We were not exactly happy travelers. We were in the middle of nowhere, wishing we were home. By now it was midafternoon, we had already come a long way, and we had no desire to return to blocked channels and inaccessible supplies. Besides, how would we ever find our way in the dark? We could only keep on going.

Gene's boat chugged along through mile after mile of channel. Children, hearing the motor, stood on the banks to cheer us on. Just as the sun slipped below the horizon, Gene and I spotted a huge body of water. This couldn't be the Matamahari River, could it? Impossible! It was too big. It had to be the Bay of Bengal. Several large salt boats there were all firmly anchored. Why were their sails not raised to catch the strong ocean breeze? Why were they not moving swiftly across the bay on their way to Cox's Bazar?

Gene pulled up next to a salt boat to ask directions to the Matamahari River. The crew looked at him as though he were retarded or crazy. "You want to cross the bay now, *Sahib* (sir)? That is quite impossible. The waves are high and the winds are treacherous. It would be too dangerous. You must wait until sunrise. Then it will be perfectly safe." They nodded sagely and pointed to the choppy waves and Gene's small boat.

My heart sank to my sandals. How could I, a lone female, stay overnight on the tiny boat with Gene and his Bengali friends? *It's impossible,* I thought mutinously. *I can't do it!* I looked at the muddy banks on our side of the channel. It looked as if we would all spend a very uncomfortable night. I was right about that, but for reasons other than what I envisioned.

One of the larger salt boats offered Gene and me hospitality for the night. The two Bengali men would sleep in Gene's motorboat and guard our supplies. I groaned inwardly. This salt boat's crew consisted of seven Muslim men. The captain looked at me, then turned and spoke to Gene, "Tell the *Memsahib* (Mrs.) she must not worry. We will take good care of you both. There are pirates in the bay, but tell her not to be afraid. We are well armed."

I'm sure he meant to be reassuring, but his words did little to ease my mind. Obviously they mistook me for Gene's wife, and we decided not to correct them. I was safer if the sailors thought I was under his protection. As Gene and I sat on the deck, one of the crew brought us rice and pungent curry made from dried fish. I was hungry but found it hard to concentrate on the food when huge cockroaches crept as close to my plate as they dared.

After dinner, Gene and I sang some Christian songs in Bengali for our hosts. The crew asked many questions, mostly about our homeland and why we now lived in East Pakistan. At bedtime, the captain gave Gene his bed, a large, raised shelf outside the boat's tiny cabin. I, being a mere woman, spread my bedding on the floor next to Gene's shelf. The crew stretched out on the deck. The captain posted an armed guard to watch for pirates.

This ship was no exception to the lack of restrooms on this ill-fated trip. The "head" consisted of a bamboo box, hanging off the stern of the boat over the ocean. The floor—if you could call it that—was a narrow border of wood, with a square hole in the center. A misstep meant a plummet into the ocean. I finally woke Gene and said, "I'm sorry to waken you, but would you *please* check out the facilities. I'm afraid I'll fall in the ocean, and I can't swim."

Gene very kindly checked everything out and told me not to worry. "The board is wide enough to stand on," he reported, chuckling. "If you're careful, you won't land in the ocean. And if you do fall in, we'll fish you out." That was small relief!

Gene and I had brought bedrolls with us, so my bed on the floor was fairly comfortable. But I still didn't get much sleep. I was definitely not accustomed to cockroaches racing up and down the floor next to my head. Gene and I were glad when morning came so we could resume our journey. After the crew served us a breakfast of bread, eggs, and tea, the captain sent us on our way with many good wishes for a safe trip.

By the time we crossed the strip of ocean and entered the mouth of the Matamahari River, we were soaked. It really *was* ocean, and the choppy waves sent sheets of salt spray across our bow and into our laps. We were happy to reach the comparative quiet of the Matamahari River. However, we soon faced another problem. The water in the river was so low that the speedboat's engine kept getting caught in the shallow spots. I became an expert at finding the deep channel. Every time I stepped off the side of the boat to look for deep water, I found myself submerged up to my waist.

The special engine Gene was trying out was supposedly designed to keep us zooming along on top of the water. Perhaps it worked better in other places, like the Florida Everglades, than it did in the shallows of the Matamahari, because it certainly didn't work for us. All it did was make us feel rather foolish. Our noisy engine ran at full throttle, yet country boats glided by us on either side, effortlessly poled by Bengali men and boys. We must have given them a good laugh in the *bazar*.

The sun went down, and still we traveled on. Gene gave up on the noisy motor and we both rowed. We had to get home, even if we rowed all night! Finally, we arrived at Lama Bazar. Gene and I had seen enough rivers, channels, and boats to last us the rest of our lives. We got out of the boat and told the Bengali men to pole it home in the morning. We would walk from there. Night had fallen, but Gene and I were armed with flashlights. Hebron station was only a mile or two from Lama Bazar—a short walk after what we'd been through! We were salty, sandy, tired, and hungry.

There they were at last—the lights of home. What an adventure! What a wonderful, "quick" trip by speedboat! Memories are made of adventures like this.

nine

The Roaring Lion

The reality of satanic oppression sometimes takes new missionaries by surprise. Most of us first learn about satanic wiles in church or at a Bible college, as missionaries from exotic lands speak compellingly about Satan's power. Hearing about that power is one thing; experiencing it is something else. When missionaries first arrived in East Pakistan, Satan had a vital interest in removing them from the scene as quickly as possible, and he worked hard to achieve his objective.

Various woes plague new missionaries in developing countries. All kinds of diseases lie in wait: malaria, amoeba, typhoid, tuberculosis, tetanus, and rabies—any one of which could prove fatal.

Road hazards abound, all of them harrowing in the extreme. Potholes draw rickshaws like magnets. Bridges washed out by torrential rains wait around blind curves. Trucks and buses thunder down the middle of the road, crowding oncoming vehicles to the edge of a ditch or embankment.

Poisonous snakes, rabid dogs, and trumpeting elephants also demonstrate their own brand of danger to the unwary. Then there are fires, floods, and cyclones—all of which have the power to wound, maim, or kill.

But wait, you say, *you're a missionary! Are missionaries not protected from all these hazards? After all, you do the Lord's work, don't you?* Yes, the Lord *does* protect in many hazardous situations, though He's not obligated to do so. Missionaries, like anyone else, must realize that Satan has certain powers and uses them whenever he has opportunity.

God watches His children closely; nothing comes into our lives except through His hands and by His permission. But God does allow difficulties in order to spiritually strengthen and mature us. We go into battle dressed in spiritual armor, but we must not advance in our own strength, or presumptuously—not ever.

New missionaries, unfamiliar with the wiles of the devil, and with limited battle experience, are especially vulnerable to Satan's frightening roar. All of us in East Pakistan were aware of his evil attacks, but their viciousness sometimes took us by surprise.

During ABWE's early years in East Pakistan, we endured frequent bouts of illness. It takes the body a long time to adjust to new foods, new germs, and a debilitating climate. Continued, prolonged illness can be depressing. Interpersonal problems may wound and weaken us, giving Satan a foothold.

One day while shopping in Cox's Bazar, I was looking for a special sleeping mat used primarily during the hot season. A friend had told me that such a mat stayed cool, even on the hottest night. I found the shop, stepped in the doorway, and asked the shopkeeper to show me a selection of woven mats. Suddenly, I was assailed by an overwhelming consciousness of evil. A Hindu holy man sat just inside the door, and evil virtually emanated from the shop. It was so frightening that I turned and fled. Never before had I sensed the presence of such palpable evil.

Gene and Beth Gurganus, taking a day off from the pressures of life in Chittagong, drove their jeep to Cox's Bazar for a day of relaxation. Beth was expecting their second baby at the time. While they were driving along the beach, the jeep hit a sinkhole in the sand. Gene and Beth escaped unharmed, but the jeep sank like a stone. The tide flowed over it three times before Gene and his helpers could extricate it.

When they returned to Chittagong, Gene, Beth, Juanita, and I sat down together and looked seriously at what was happening to us. Sickness, a colleague's death, interpersonal conflicts, riot, culture shock, and frequent catastrophic events beyond our control made us feel that we were under an intense attack of Satan. Lydia, listening quietly to our conversation, spoke up and said, "Please, talk about something else. I don't want to hear any more. It scares me to listen to you."

Gene responded with unusual firmness. "Lydia, we have to talk about these things. If you don't want to listen, sweetheart, just leave the room. You don't have to sit here and listen to us talk."

We declared our intention of staying in East Pakistan no matter what happened. Gene, Beth, Juanita, and I prayed together, pleading with God for an umbrella of heavenly protection. There was no turning back; we were in for the long haul. After that, the attacks eased for a time, and we were able to catch our breath.

That winter was the one in which Joyce Wingo and I moved to Hebron, where I reopened Helen Miller's medical dispensary so I could help the Bengalis and tribal people who lived in the area, and Joyce began her translation work. Living arrangements were primitive and the work was difficult. I suffered periodic bouts of amoebic dysentery, which wore me down physically. The medicine gave me double vision and insomnia, among other things. If I wanted to read, I had to cover one eye just to see the print clearly. The cure was almost worse than the disease.

Because we lived on the edge of deep jungle at Hebron, mosquitoes were a real trial. It was almost impossible to keep them out of our bamboo houses. Like squadrons of fighter planes zooming in for attack, they arrived every afternoon at dusk. I finally made a mosquito net big enough to cover a deck chair, a small table, and a kerosene lamp. It became my refuge after clinic hours. Despite the mosquito net, I still experienced periodic bouts of malaria. Malaria gave me severe photophobia (sensitivity to light) and terrible headaches. Even the melodic clank of cowbells was enough to set my teeth on edge.

Satan is no gentleman. He waits until we are weakened by disease or depression to launch a nasty attack. I had been sick for several weeks with what seemed to be amoebic hepatitis, and nothing I tried seemed to help. I just could not get over it, and Satan had a field day. Some nights it was as if all the demons of hell mocked around my bed. Intense, prolonged prayer was my only weapon to drive them away. It was both frightening and demoralizing.

Satan then began to whisper a suggestion in my ear. He told me repeatedly that I was not going to recover; I would die. But that wasn't all. I would be buried before I was dead! Everyone would think I was dead, but I would still be alive. Worst of all, my colleagues would bury me, convinced that I had already died. I wasn't afraid to die—I knew I would go to heaven—but I just could not imagine being buried alive. It sounds weird now, but at the time it was both real and very frightening.

Joyce's little bamboo house stood opposite mine. When I finally went to her and told her what was happening, she didn't laugh at me. Her face reflected the horror I felt. "Joyce," I pleaded, "*please* promise me you won't let anyone bury me unless you know I'm dead. Please!"

If she thought I was losing my grip on reality she didn't show it. "First of all," Joyce replied, "I don't believe you're going to die. You only feel this way because you've been ill. But I promise you that if you *do* die, I'll make certain you're dead before anyone lays a finger on you. Stop worrying about it." That put an end to my fears and Satan's evil suggestion.

Lydia Gurganus was extremely ill with repeated lung infections during that first term. Whenever she had severe bronchitis, Gene and Beth took her to Chandraghona Hospital to see the British mission doctor. Dr. Bottoms treated Lydia and got her back on her feet—until the next time she got sick. He could not seem to find the precipitating factor in her frequent illnesses. Finally, Dr. Bottoms said, "If you don't get Lydia out of this country, you're going to lose her, probably to tuberculosis. Take her to America and find someone who can diagnose and treat her illness properly!"

The departure of Beth Gurganus and their little girls was a big blow to the missionaries. Paul Miller and Mary Barnard had died; Victor and Winnifred Barnard were preparing for furlough; and Helen Miller was taking her children home to America. Now Beth and the girls had to leave, too. Joyce and I knew the ABWE board would never consent to us living alone in Hebron or Chittagong without the presence of at least one male missionary. Gene wanted desperately to accompany his family, but couldn't bear to see the Hebron work close down. He put his family on a plane for North Carolina, while he stayed on until someone came to help man the Hebron station. Gene was desperately lonely without his family, but he was determined to stay at Hebron as long as necessary.

These missionary families were leaving less than five years after opening the work in East Pakistan. We had won a few skirmishes, but had Satan won the war? Without reinforcements, we could not go on. It looked as though everything was coming to an end almost before it had begun. What would happen to our plans for Bengali and tribal evangelism now?

Then, in 1960, Jay and Eleanor Walsh willingly stepped into the breach and moved to Hebron at that crucial moment. They worked against almost impossible odds to keep Hebron and the work in East Pakistan going until the Olsens and other missionaries appeared on the scene. The tribal work continued. Satan lost that round.

Satanic oppression in Chittagong was real, but those who worked at Hebron felt an almost overwhelming force of satanic opposition. Chittagong had a bit of spiritual enlightenment, and Satan's power was not as easily discerned in the big city. But the small villages near Hebron and the surrounding hill tracts had been steeped in satanic darkness for generations. Satan had no intention of giving up even one inch of ground to the children of Light. He fought us every step of the way.

We saw some Bengalis saved because of the mission work at Hebron, but the greatest spiritual fruit came from among the tribal people, who were uniquely prepared for the gospel. They often made animal sacrifices to protect themselves from Satan and his demonic forces, believing that the sacrificial blood covered them and made it impossible for Satan to see them. When they learned that the blood of Jesus Christ did more than protect them from Satan, they wanted to know more. The tribal people discovered that Christ's sacrifice could actually take away their sins and free them from Satan's grip on their lives. When the light of the gospel enlightened their minds, we often saw entire villages turn from spirit worship to follow Christ.

Years of soil preparation, sowing, and cultivation passed before we saw lasting fruit among the Bengalis at Hebron. In the late 1970s, the government forced the Hebron station to close because it was no longer considered a safe place for foreigners. Some of our missionaries there were caught in the crossfire between feuding tribal people and the Bengali government. Certain tribes wanted more autonomy, but the government was reluctant to comply with their demands. It also appeared as though foreign insurgents might be helping the warring tribes. In light of this situation, the government decided it could no longer assure the safety of foreign nationals.

Missionaries still are not permitted to live at Hebron, but they are allowed to visit with permission. Christian tribal workers teach and preach God's Word, and Hebron serves as a center for tribal seminars and conferences. These well-trained Christian leaders are teaching a second and even a third generation to reach their own people with the gospel. People are still being saved because of Hebron's influence on the Belchari community.

Missionaries who worked at Hebron in the early days sacrificed a great deal to keep it open. They showed God's love to their neighbors, helped the sick and poor, and brought the gospel to sin-scarred Bengalis and tribal people. I'm sure that Satan rues the day missionaries established Hebron and claimed that beautiful region for Christ.

t e n

My Shepherd

My mother always supported my desire to know God and follow His will. My father, however, wonderful man that he was, was anxious to see me settled. He thought I should study something *practical*. "That way, you will always have financial security," he said. *Practical,* in his mind, meant a secretarial course, a prospect that held no interest for me. Dad knew that nurse's training would be expensive, and the training itself long and difficult. He thought secretaries didn't have to work such long hours or perform such unpleasant, demeaning tasks as nurses. But God made it possible for me to study nursing, and I thought nursing skills would prove valuable on the mission field.

My father's health continued to deteriorate during my nurse's training, and he died just a few weeks before my graduation. I am grateful for the support and encouragement of my family throughout my training. It was a proud and happy day when I donned my white uniform and cap and received my pin at Rochester's citywide graduation exercises.

After I was appointed by ABWE as a missionary to East Pakistan, Mother and I shared an apartment while I raised support—a process known then as deputation—and worked part time at Highland Hospital. We enjoyed that time together, in spite of my impending departure. I know that thinking about the long separation caused Mother grief, but she never expressed her sorrow. Instead, she encouraged me whenever she could.

After I sailed from New York for East Pakistan, Mother moved in with my brother Walt, who also lived in Rochester.

Mom faithfully wrote every week while I lived in East Pakistan, keeping me updated on family news. When a Canadian relative died during my first term, Mother inherited her quaint old house in Frankford, Ontario. Mom finally owned the home she had always wanted.

My sister Nina and her family, on furlough from missionary work in Central Africa, looked forward to spending time with Mother in Canada, and Mother was busy getting everything ready for their visit. During this time, Mom's neighbor Margaret stopped by to visit, along with another friend who was a nurse. While they sat talking in the parlor, Mother collapsed, and the nurse quickly called an ambulance.

Margaret called my brother Walt, who drove to Canada immediately, where the doctor told him that Mother had suffered a stroke. She was unconscious, but in stable condition. Although the doctor was optimistic, that night Mom suffered another major stroke and slipped quietly into heaven. The rest of the family gathered in Rochester for her funeral. I was too far away to return.

That was 1960, and I was in Dacca, the capital of East Pakistan, being treated for persistent amoebic dysentery. When I returned to Chittagong, Joyce met me at the mission guesthouse and broke the news as gently as possible. She showed me the cable from home that gave the news of Mother's sudden death.

Actually, God had prepared me for my parents' deaths while I was attending Bible school. One day He simply asked me to give my parents into His keeping. It was as though He said, "I'm not taking them away now, but I want you to give them to Me." It was a long time before I could honestly put them in His hands. Now they were both in His hands for eternity.

Major Oliver Omerod, hearing of my loss, invited Joyce and me to stay at his home, a big old house owned by the railway company and situated high on a hill overlooking Chittagong. Oliver took good care of us, and his quiet, comfortable home gave me the peace I needed.

One afternoon, Oliver told us there would be a service at the Anglican church that evening. "Why don't you and Joyce go with me?" he suggested. "The Scottish pastor from Calcutta is visiting Chittagong, and he will conduct the service." Joyce and I agreed that we would enjoy attending a worship service in English.

Every seat in beautiful Christ Church was occupied. It looked as though everyone who spoke English attended. The Scottish pastor was a cheerful little man who obviously loved God and His Word. When the congregation sang beloved old hymns, the sound almost lifted the roof off the building. The atmosphere, in marked contrast to the usual somber services held in this church, was joyful and buoyant, a time of fellowship that lifted our spirits and filled us with gladness at God's goodness and mercy.

In that brief hour, I felt as though God had planned that service just for me. I could not attend Mother's funeral, but this was a service she would have loved. The congregation sang David Grant's moving Scottish version of Psalm 23:

> The Lord's my Shepherd, I'll not want;
> He makes me down to lie
> In pastures green He leadeth me
> The quiet waters by.
>
> My soul He doth restore again;
> And me to walk doth make
> Within the paths of righteousness,
> E'en for His own name's sake.
>
> Yea, though I walk through death's dark vale,
> Yet will I fear no ill;
> For Thou art with me, and Thy rod
> And staff me comfort still.
>
> My table Thou hast furnished
> In presence of my foes;
> My head Thou dost with oil anoint,
> And my cup overflows.

Goodness and mercy all my life
Shall surely follow me;
And in God's house forevermore
My dwelling place shall be.

—*David Grant (1833–1893)*

This ancient psalm, sung with great joy, served as my eulogy for Mother. God's house was now her dwelling place, and I was content to have her there.

Whenever I hear David Grant's hymn sung or read, it reminds me that Mother is in heaven and our joyful reunion lies ahead. Mother loved beauty, and I'm sure that heaven's beauty is more than she ever imagined.

eleven

Lesson from an Avocado Tree

Trees take a long time to bear fruit, and we found that it took an equally long time to produce spiritual fruit in East Pakistan. In the early days it seemed as though all our efforts came to nothing. We had invaded Satan's territory. If we expected him to turn and flee at our approach, we were sadly mistaken. Perhaps we were not sufficiently prepared for the intensity of the spiritual battle we faced. I had always thought of Africa as the "Dark Continent," but the Indian sub-continent, which included East Pakistan, was every bit as dark as Africa. Whenever a Bengali showed the tiniest flicker of interest in the gospel, Satan quickly extinguished the spark. Inevitably, we found ourselves plunged back into the black night of spiritual darkness.

If you have ever seen farmland during an extended drought, you know that such soil is hard and unyielding. Rice fields, soft and pliable during the rainy season, become hard as rock during the long dry season. The Barnards and the Millers, Gene Gurganus, Jay and Eleanor Walsh, Joyce Wingo, and I, along with the missionaries who followed us at Hebron, cleared spiritual fields, broke up the hard lumps, watered the soil with our tears, firmly planted God's Word, and waited for a harvest. We had to wait a long time.

In the area around Hebron, most ethnic Bengalis professed Buddhism, with Hinduism and animism entwined like a resistant vine. Tribal people were outright animists who made blood sacrifices to protect themselves from demonic power. Satan had done his best to delude and entrap these people. No one challenged his ownership of them until Christian missionaries appeared on the scene.

Missionaries recognized the spiritual darkness at Hebron, but it was always a surprise when the Bengalis echoed our sentiments. Our neighbors in Belchari often said, "When you are here, it is light. When you get in your boat and go downriver, the light goes out. We are surrounded by darkness."

Christ said, "I will build my church and the gates of hell shall not prevail against it" (Matthew 16:18). This verse takes on new meaning in the context of people held captive by Satan's lies. Only the power of God can snatch people from Satan's hand and set them firmly on the road to heaven. Christ had to build His church through the power of the Holy Spirit and the illumination of His Word. But we could depend on the truth of God's promise in Matthew 16:18. He *would* build His church, but in His own way and in His time.

When I first began to teach Bible stories to teenage Bengali girls at Hebron, I was unopposed. The girls' families allowed them to come to my house whenever I was free to teach them. This attitude changed abruptly, however, when I began teaching Bible verses during sewing class. I promised to teach them a Bible verse every week, and as we worked on our sewing project, we reviewed Bible verses aloud. None of the girls could read, so they had to commit each verse to memory. I was amazed at how hard they tried and how quickly they learned.

Memorizing God's Word was the cut-off point. Once I began to teach Bible verses, the girls were no longer permitted to come to my house. There was always work for them to do at home, or something came up at the last minute. Satan's obvious ploy was nonetheless devastating. He quickly plucked God's Word out of the girls' hearts. Classes came to an abrupt halt, at least for the time being.

While Jay and Eleanor Walsh, Joyce, and I lived at Hebron, the building of Kaptai Dam to the north forced thousands of

Bengalis to abandon houses, fields, and gardens, and to relocate in distant, unpopulated areas designated by the government. Virtually overnight, a new village sprang up across the river from Hebron station. To induce the Bengalis to move, the government of Pakistan made these people many promises. But the dislocated Bengalis soon discovered that they must build their own houses, prepare their fields, and plant their gardens—without the promised help.

This was hard work in a new, totally uncultivated area. But a river ran along one side of the new village, giving the residents year-round access to water that would help maintain their crops and gardens. The newcomers settled in quickly, built bamboo houses, planted tiny gardens, and prepared to plant rice in the rainy season.

The Walshes and Joyce and I soon got to know our neighbors, since they often came to Hebron for medicine or other assistance. Jay visited their village and enjoyed good rapport with many of the residents. We became friends with Debindra, a Hindu laundryman and his family. Laundry workers are considered low caste, but serve an important function in any village. They wash, dry, starch, and iron clothes for anyone able to pay the small fee for their services.

I got to know Debindra's wife, Promilla, and their children. One day Promilla brought their beautiful little girl, Preeti, to my clinic for treatment. She was unconscious, but I cherished hope that Preeti's illness was treatable. I routinely gave an injection of anti-malarial medicine because children with malaria responded to it so quickly. The injection had little effect, however, and there was little else to do for an unconscious child. I cared for Preeti in the clinic day and night. The tiny flame of life finally flickered out, and her family prepared to take her home for burial. It was heartbreaking to hear Promilla singing a death chant as she trudged home across the fields, beating her chest with her fists. She loved her little daughter so much, and the child's death was a bitter loss. In spite of the family's grief, they were grateful for our care of Preeti in her final illness.

Eventually, the seed we sowed began to sprout. One by one, Debindra's family members were saved, as God's Word took root in their hearts. Promilla was steeped in Hinduism, and it took her a long time to understand the gospel. After she accepted Christ and was baptized, Promilla said, "I really didn't know much when I accepted Christ, but I believed you when you said He would save me from my sins if I trusted Him. As I went to church with my husband and heard messages from God's Word, I slowly began to understand who God really is and what He did for me."

We often heard statements like Promilla's. The desire to know God was the spark that led to understanding, and, gradually, Satan's hold on some of these people was broken. Many believers emerged from those early days at Hebron. Now some of their sons and daughters are believers, teaching a new generation of children to know and love God. It was a long, hard struggle, but a wonderful victory when the missionaries finally saw fruit.

When Khoka worked with me in the clinic, he kept me apprised of what was happening in Belchari village. It did not sound like a happy place to live. He usually had at least one story to tell about a husband who beat his wife. Spousal abuse was a way of life for many of these women who were becoming my friends. They came often to the clinic for medicine for themselves and their children. Some were the teenage girls I had taught in Bible classes. All lived in grinding poverty, but they loved their children and tried to take good care of them. I protested, "But Khoka, why did he beat her? She's so sweet! I can't imagine her doing anything that deserves a beating."

Khoka's usual answer was, "Why did he beat her? He beat her to keep her good, that's why! A wife won't stay good unless you beat her once in awhile." I couldn't understand that reasoning. Perhaps beatings kept the wives submissive, but they obeyed out of fear, not love.

In Hindu marriages and within the Buddhist community at Hebron, the husband becomes the wife's god. Complete obedience and total submission to her husband are part of her wedding vows. Khoka once told me about a village woman whose husband had beaten her badly. When I asked the reason, he said, "She was nursing the baby when her husband told her to go and weed the chili peppers. She told him she would do it as soon as she finished feeding the baby. It was foolish of her to say that because it really made him angry. She should have gone immediately."

Because the husband's word is law, the wife's family hesitates to interfere, even when they know their daughter is being abused. It is not unusual for a father to send his daughter back to her husband's home, even though she has run away because of physical abuse. Many young wives committed suicide, believing it was their only escape from an intolerable marriage.

In that part of the world, it is customary for a son to bring his new bride home to live with his family. When a family has several sons and each brings his bride home to live, the house must expand to accommodate the new family. The bride and groom may be assigned a room of their own in his father's house, or the father may build an additional sleeping room for the new bride and groom.

Sometimes a young man takes a bride because his mother needs help with the cooking and housework. However, the mother-in-law may make life miserable for her new daughter-in-law. It is not unusual for a mother-in-law to turn her son against the bride, or to insist that he beat his wife for a minor offense. Perhaps the young wife's cooking isn't up to her mother-in-law's standards; she doesn't move quickly enough; or she cries because she is homesick for her parents. The stories that came out of the villages near Hebron made me heartsick.

Once the gospel penetrated hearts, wonderful changes took place in individuals and families. Instead of fear and alienation, love and acceptance blossomed. But it took time to weed out sins such as wife beating. Many evils that seemed acceptable when heathen couples married were unacceptable when Christians married. Sometimes new believers faced difficulty in comprehending how marriage is supposed to mirror the love Christ has for His church.

On my way back to East Pakistan for my second term, I visited my sister Nina in Central Africa, where she and her family worked for more than twenty years. The churches were full, with strong, national leaders, and Christian families were teaching the next generation to follow the Lord. Years of missionary endeavor had borne much lasting fruit.

While in Central Africa, I collected some souvenirs to take back to East Pakistan. One of the missionary ladies raised magnificent African violets. I put leaves from the prettiest plants in a small plastic box, where I could keep them moist. I would plant them when I got back to East Pakistan. I also put an avocado pit in a small tin can. I thought it would be fun to grow avocados at Hebron.

I returned to Hebron for a brief visit and planted the avocado pit on a hillside near my house. Then I forgot all about it. I lived in Chittagong for most of my second term, raising a girl named Shabi, teaching missionary kids, and working on Bengali literature preparation.

Several years later, Shirley Harkness, a missionary schoolteacher, returned to Malumghat after a visit to Hebron. "Is it possible," she asked, "that there is an avocado tree at Hebron? A tree on the hillside near your old house is covered with knobby fruit that look like avocados."

"Shirley," I said, "I planted an avocado pit on that hillside such a long time ago I had forgotten all about it. If they *are* avocados, they must be from that pit I brought from Africa."

Had that avocado pit actually borne fruit? The next time a missionary made a trip to Hebron, she brought back a huge basket of knobby, dark green African avocados. Those who enjoy the fruit, especially missionaries from California, were elated at this unexpected windfall.

It was a good reminder for me that fruit trees eventually bear fruit. God had promised a spiritual harvest at Hebron; He just didn't tell the missionaries how long it would take. Sometimes it takes many years to produce lasting fruit, but fruit that remains through drought and storm is worth waiting for. The magnificent spiritual fruit harvested from those early days at Hebron will be our joy and crown through all eternity.

twelve

Samaritan Woman

Shabitri Barua was one of the first people I met when I moved to Hebron. A petite, vivacious girl of perhaps thirteen or fourteen years of age, she walked to the mission station from her father's home in Belchari village to see if I had any work she could do. A houseboy carried water from the well and helped with the cleaning, cooking, and washing, so I did not need Shabitri's help in my house. Instead, she performed odd jobs in the garden. Shabitri, also known as Shabi, possessed a lively curiosity about the strange white foreigners who had moved into her area. She had known the Barnard and Miller families when they lived at Hebron, and now she had to get used to a new group of strangers. Shabi was friendly and outgoing, so no one remained a stranger for long.

Before Jay Walsh built a small clinic for me, I examined patients on my verandah. This was far from ideal, because patients dropped by my house anytime, day or night. Medical help was scarce between Hebron and Chittagong, and Chittagong was more than a day's journey by boat and bus. The closest medical facility, at Lama Bazar, was within walking distance, but local people complained that the government medical officer had almost no medicine. The mission clinic at Hebron was not well equipped, but I could treat most common complaints. Medicine was readily available in Chittagong, and I kept a good supply on hand because I knew that asking a patient to go to Chittagong for treatment was like asking him to go to the moon! Most Belchari villagers had never even traveled to Cheringha, a town only a few miles away and easily reachable by country boat. Men from Belchari frequented the local markets, held in the surrounding towns on different days of the week. The women, however, had little reason to leave home except to visit friends and neighbors or find help for a sick child.

Without any roads in the area, travel in and out of Hebron was by boat or on foot. Moghs, Murungs, and Tipperahs brought food and baskets from their hill tribes to sell at Lama Bazar, where they bought items like salt and matches to take back to their remote villages. Many tribal people stopped by my clinic for medicine on *bazar* days, since it was on their route to Lama Bazar. But tribal people don't mind walking long distances, so they came for medicine anytime they needed it. I also treated more than my fair share of emergency cases. The clinic was a busy place that gave the missionaries at Hebron a good outreach into the community.

Shabi frequented the clinic, mostly out of curiosity. She loved to hear stories, and I told her Bible stories whenever I had time. Religion in Belchari was a strange mixture of Hinduism and Buddhism, and I found it frustrating that Shabi equated Bible stories with the tales of Hindu deities she had heard from childhood. She was illiterate, and she believed anything she heard. My assistant, Khoka, often talked to her at length, and it was he who told me about her family.

Shabi lived on the edge of Belchari village with her father, stepmother, and young half brother. Her father farmed a bit of land, but the family was very poor. Even though Shabi had virtually no schooling, she seemed intelligent. She regularly attended the Buddhist temple with her family. She loved the Buddhist festivals, when village girls dressed in their best clothes and took offerings of rice, fruit, and flowers to the temple. Because she loved stories, Shabi talked me into starting an evening Bible class with her friends. I wasn't sure it was a good idea. Considerable hostility surfaced when I had started a class earlier, but Shabi insisted we try it again. If I would shepherd the girls home afterwards, she would help round them up for class.

Watching her gather her friends for class was revealing. I mentally called her the "Samaritan woman," thinking of the way in which the Samaritan woman in the Bible told all of her friends about meeting Jesus. I would drop off my teaching materials and kerosene lantern at the clinic before meeting Shabi at her house. Then we tramped from house to house, calling the girls. Shabi would slide back the bamboo door and say the equivalent of "My goodness, aren't you ready yet? Hurry up, the *Missahib* is waiting!" Then Shabi prodded her friend along until we were ready to go on to the next house. Here she repeated her urging until, finally, seven or eight of us were walking back to the clinic in the fading light.

I prayed a great deal about the lessons I taught. It is extremely difficult to teach spiritual truths to those with no background in Christianity. The leap of faith from darkness to light is huge. The stories I told were not myths or fables, and I wanted the girls to understand that. Nor did I want them to link the truths of God's Word with the tales they heard in the Buddhist temple. Only God could bridge the huge gap between my teaching and their understanding.

Whenever I reviewed a lesson in class, Shabi offered the most feedback. She usually recalled the main points of a lesson without hesitation. Often, she could also apply its truths to her own life situation. Bengalis have wonderful memories, but they often find it hard to put what they have memorized to practical use. Yet somehow, spiritual truth was impacting Shabi's life. Would the Holy Spirit enlighten her spiritual darkness and give her understanding? This was my prayer for Shabi.

After class I lit my kerosene lantern, locked the clinic door, and walked the girls back to their homes along the village path. Shabi was the last one I dropped off, at her father's house, before walking across the fields to my own house. A special Muslim friend of mine lived close to the trail outside Belchari village in a tiny house with her son, Abra. A quiet, sweet lady with a quick smile and gentle ways, she was known as Abrar Ma (Abra's mother). After I dropped off Shabi at her house, my homeward path took me past Abrar Ma's house. On cold winter nights, she watched for me and called to me. While I waited for her on the footpath, she ran out to slip into my hand a warm sweet potato she had baked in hot coals. Abrar Ma always timed it perfectly. The potato was always well cooked but never too hot to handle. Even with the skin on, the potato was delicious. Abrar Ma's kind, generous gesture warmed me up for the walk home.

As often as possible, I prepared visuals for the Bible stories I told. I drew pictures, illustrating the story of Christ and the two thieves who died with Him. It was important for the girls to understand the difference in the thieves' response to Christ. I wanted them to see that Jesus Christ could take away their sins and give them His righteousness. Shabi understood the lesson immediately. During review time, she retold the story in great detail. I held my breath. Was the gospel real to her at last?

After we reviewed the story several times in class, Shabi came to my house for a visit. We sat and chatted for a few minutes, then I asked her about some things Khoka had told me regarding her involvement with young men in the village. Were these things true? "Oh, *Missahib*," she said, "you know the people in the village! They don't like it that I come to your house all the time. They're trying to get me in trouble so you won't let me come here anymore.

"But," she continued, "I came to ask you something. You know that story you told us—the one about Jesus and the two thieves? Do you think that when God looks at me, my heart looks like that black one you showed us?"

"Shabi," I said, "you know what God sees when He looks at your heart. Is your heart full of sin? Is that what God sees when He looks at you?"

Shabi thought about that for a long time. Living in the village, she knew a great deal about sin. Whether the villagers were telling the truth about her or not, she knew she was a sinful person. Finally, she said, "Yes, I'm sure that's what God sees when He looks at my heart. I really would like to have a clean heart like the one God gave the other thief. Do you think God would do that for me? Would He take my black heart and give me His white one?"

I was thrilled that Shabi finally understood what God had done for her. Only He could have given her this understanding. "Shabi," I said, "of course He would! He'd be happy to take away your sins and give you a clean heart. All you have to do is tell Him what you've told me. If you want to, you can do that right now."

Shabi and I prayed together. She told God she knew her heart was black with sin. She asked Him to take away her sins and give her His clean, white heart. We talked about what she had done. I told her I would pray for her and teach her more about God and His Word. Her understanding of spiritual truth was limited, but God's Holy Spirit, living within her, would teach her all she needed to know. Of all the girls in that class, Shabi was the one who made a firm commitment to Christ—and stood fast.

Following her confession of faith, Shabi went through severe persecution because she was not the kind of person to keep the good news to herself. She had to tell people that God had forgiven all her sins. Her family was furious. Shabi, a Christian? How could this have happened? Her parents would lose face in the community, and they hated that more than anything. How could the family stand the disgrace? Excommunication is usually the first response when a heathen embraces Christianity. Shabi lost her place in her family and in the Buddhist community and temple, although her father allowed her to live on a tiny verandah at one end of the house. He gave her a blanket and a cooking pot. From now on she must find her own food and take care of herself. She was on her own.

Shabi's father forbade her to visit my house. Her family held me responsible for her conversion. They thought that if she got hungry enough, she'd recant her newfound faith and return to the Buddhist community. I often met Shabi on the riverbank and gave her bread, fruit, or rice so she'd have something to eat. Being rejected by her family and also isolated from her friends made her sad, but she never complained of being cold, hungry, or discouraged.

Shabi's one great fear, being of marriageable age, was that her family would make good on their threat to marry her to a Buddhist. Shabi knew that if she married a Buddhist, she would find it almost impossible to live as a Christian. Life was hard enough now. What would it be like with an unbelieving husband?

A few months after Shabi's salvation, I left East Pakistan for furlough in the United States. I planned to return to Hebron after furlough. However, by the time I returned, the situation among the missionaries was changing. ABWE now planned to build a hospital south of Chittagong. A medical team was assembled and many decisions required our undivided attention. The field council decided that all the nurses should live in Chittagong until the hospital was built, then the medical personnel would move to the hospital together. Meanwhile, there were building plans to finalize and other important decisions about the medical work to make. It was a cooperative effort, and everyone—including me—needed to be involved in planning and preparation.

When I returned from furlough, I visited briefly at Hebron and told Shabi about my plans. She was devastated by the news that I was moving to Chittagong. "Please, *Missahib*," she pleaded, "take me with you. If I stay here, my family will marry me to a Buddhist. If they do, I'll never be able to live as a Christian. If you leave, who will teach me about the Bible? Can't you make room for me in Chittagong?"

Looking back, I can hardly imagine the courage it took for her to make this request. Shabi had always lived in a small village. The city of Chittagong was huge by comparison and far from her home. Yet she trusted God enough to break away from everything familiar in order to live as a believer. Perhaps this girl I had thought of as the "Samaritan woman" was more akin to a Rahab or a Ruth.

"Shabi," I said, "I just don't know how I can do what you've asked. I'm sure your father wouldn't let me take you away from Belchari village, and I don't think there's room for you in the missionary nurses' house. I have to ask permission from the other missionaries to take you out of your village, and I honestly think they would refuse. But you can do one thing—pray and ask God to do whatever pleases Him. If this is what He wants for you, He can make all the arrangements. I'll pray, too, and ask God to help us know His will."

Frankly, I foresaw nothing but obstacles. The field council did not encourage national believers to break away from their families. Why would they approve Shabi's request? Besides, Shabi's father and stepmother had plans for her future. I was the "bad guy" who taught Shabi to turn her back on Buddhism and caused her family's loss of face in the village.

In Chittagong, the missionary nurses had rented a house, which they were preparing for occupancy. If Shabi lived with me, I'd have to locate an apartment. I also needed someone to live with me and share responsibility for Shabi's care. How could I possibly work out all the details? Even praying about it was a giant step of faith for both of us. But if God worked out the seemingly impossible details, I would keep my promise to take her away from Belchari.

God cleared away the obstacles so quickly it made my head spin. After my visit to Hebron, I returned to Chittagong and told the other nurses my story. Becky Davey, one of the new nurses planning to move to the nearly completed mission hospital, thought the idea was a great one. Although still in language study, Becky offered to share an apartment and help care for Shabi if we received permission to bring her to Chittagong.

Becky and I nervously approached the field council, explaining that, if Shabi remained in Belchari, her family would undoubtedly marry her to a Buddhist. Considerable discussion followed our bold proposal, but the field council vote was in our favor, and our colleagues gave us their blessing. We prayed together as a group and asked God to help us remove Shabi from her village.

Lynn Silvernale lived in Hebron at that time, so Becky and I asked her to talk to Shabi's father. We wanted him to understand that Becky and I would care for his daughter and pay all her expenses. Ours was not a bid to adopt her, but we wanted to "borrow" Shabi for an extended period of time. I think her father saw our proposal as a way out of his difficulty. He loved Shabi but could not stand the intense pressure put on him by the village elders. He knew that if his daughter stayed in Belchari, he must bow to the will of the community and arrange a Buddhist marriage for her. A poor man, his daughter's wedding would place him in debt for the rest of his life. If Becky and I took Shabi off his hands now, he was "off the hook," at least for several years. He gave Lynn his consent, which she wrote in a long letter explaining what had happened.

Shabi had to be spirited out of Belchari village for her own protection. If the village leaders knew of the plans in advance, they might prevent her departure. Lynn was careful to involve Shabi's father in all our plans and arranged to bring Shabi with her to Chittagong the next time she came down from Hebron.

Meanwhile, Becky and I found an ideal apartment in a Bengali neighborhood. It was not only adequate, it even included a small alcove for Shabi's cot. Everything happened quickly and smoothly; it was obvious that God arranged all the details. Becky and I faced many challenges in caring for Shabi over the next few years, but she had a bright, sunny personality, and it was fun to have her as part of our home. We wanted her to be a happy, healthy Christian. Living in Chittagong, she could attend Bengali church and learn spiritual truths on a regular basis. She also learned a great deal from living with us, and Becky and I probably learned even more than she did.

Eventually, Shabi attended a Christian boarding school, where she became an excellent student. When Memorial Christian Hospital at Malumghat was completed, Shabi was excited at the opportunity to work there.

The dialect spoken at Malumghat is the same one Shabi spoke in Belchari village. To those who speak pure Bengali, the dialect's vocabulary and idiom seem hopelessly complex. But it was Shabi's mother tongue, and she enjoyed speaking it with patients at the hospital. Because of Shabi's fluency in this dialect, she was able to minister to female patients in a unique way, and she gradually worked her way into ministry as a Bible woman. Her knowledge of the Chittagonian dialect enabled her to reach out to patients and their families when no one else could. God had wonderfully prepared Shabi for this special place and ministry.

A fine young man moved to Malumghat and eventually became the pastor of the local Bengali church. Goni John—a member of the Tipperah tribe—was a gentle, refined, and well-educated young man. Dr. Michael Flowers, a British Baptist missionary, served at the Chandraghona Baptist Mission Hospital, on the same compound as the boarding school Shabi had attended. Dr. Flowers had seen Goni's potential as a teenager and had funded his education. Goni's father and stepmother, who had both had leprosy, lived in the leper colony at Chandraghona hospital for several years, but medicine had arrested their disease. Once the family was free to leave the colony, they eventually moved to Malumghat to live near their son. Goni's father worked as a gardener, and his stepmother sometimes worked as a nanny for patients or missionaries.

Goni John watched Shabi from a distance for a long time. Her happy demeanor and spirituality deeply impressed him. He knew of her difficult background but decided she would make an ideal pastor's wife. They married and became the parents of two children, a daughter, Chobhi, and a son, Uttam. Chobhi grew up to marry Ajoi, a fine Bengali pastor, and they have three children, two boys and a girl. Uttam is married to a lovely Christian tribal girl and has a young son. Becky and I are not only Shabi's foster parents, we are Chobhi and Uttam's "grandmothers" and their children's "great-grandmothers." When I first met her, Shabi was just a young, uneducated village girl. Then God reached down and saved her. Shabi's life has reached many with the story of God's love and forgiveness. His grace richly touched her life and, through her, the lives of many other Bengalis and tribal people.

thirteen

Our Extremity—God's Opportunity

There is so much about working in a mission hospital that just cannot be expressed in words: the sights, smells, sounds, and experiences that are so completely foreign to those in developed countries. I found it mind-boggling to cope with onions and potatoes stored in bedside stands, sooty cooking pots and sleeping mats stashed under patient beds, chicken bones strewn on ward floors, and live chickens that careened out of private patient rooms, squawking loudly.

I have visited mission hospitals in Africa, Brazil, Hong Kong, India, and the United Arab Emirates, and each hospital clearly showed the wealth or poverty of the particular country. Memorial Christian Hospital (MCH), opened in 1966, was one of the best medical facilities in East Pakistan. Our missionary doctors and nurses were well trained and committed to excellent patient care, and we worked hard to train our national staff to the highest possible level of proficiency.

Bob Adolph, a laboratory technologist, set up MCH's laboratory and training program, and Bengali laboratory technicians learned their craft under his personal supervision. MCH boasted its own X-ray facility. Larry Golin, newly trained in physical therapy, set up and supervised that department. Eventually, Larry and orthopedic surgeon John Bullock established the first limb and brace center in Bangladesh. As new missionary doctors arrived, the hospital added gynecology, orthopedics, and plastic surgery. I completed several months of training in dentistry during furlough, then added a much-needed dental room to service patients and staff. Of all the medical work I did on the field, dentistry was probably the most appreciated. To the patient with a bad toothache, the simple act of pulling an aching tooth was the best gift I could give, and it was good public relations for the hospital.

MCH's circle of influence grew quickly, attracting patients from as far away as Dacca to the north and Burma to the south. Rich and poor streamed through the front door, seeking medical and surgical treatment. The majority of our patients came from desperately poor homes in poverty-stricken villages. With so many patients clamoring for care, MCH's staff faced the overwhelming task of determining criteria for treatment. It was even harder to set up a sliding scale for payment, though that was absolutely necessary in order to remain financially solvent.

As the country's population increased, so did the number of patients. The medical staff sometimes felt as if they were drowning in an ever-growing stream of patients that poured through the gates and sapped hospital resources. MCH staff had to limit the number of outpatients to those we could examine, diagnose, and treat on any given day. We faced an ongoing battle to make the number of admissions equal the number of empty hospital beds. Even so, we often ran out of beds before we ran out of patients who sought admission. It was common to line up army cots for patients in the hallways or down the middle of a ward.

Deciding which outpatients could be seen was a nightmare for the nurse assigned to the job. When everyone is in desperate condition, whom do you turn away? When you have only one empty bed in a ward, how do you decide which critically ill patient will occupy it? Nurse Jean Weld did an excellent job of outpatient triage, but there were days she could barely face another patient. The load finally became so heavy, and night call so demanding, that nurse Becky Davey developed a medic program. Becky and her staff taught Bengali medics to triage patients, handle minor illnesses and emergencies, and take first night call.

This relieved some of the load of the missionaries, but it did not reduce the overall number of patients admitted to MCH.

During some seasons of the year, outpatient department (OPD) personnel treat dozens of malaria patients. Typhoid also makes fierce, periodic visits to the area. Pneumonia and burns are common in the winter. Orthopedic patients often clog the wards, and new babies and their mothers sometimes seem to occupy every available space.

While I worked as matron (director of nurses) of the hospital, MCH faced a full-blown cholera epidemic. There were so many patients that Dr. Donn Ketcham asked the Cholera Research Laboratory in Dacca for help. When they learned we were fighting an epidemic, they sent a team of specialists to assist with the care of cholera victims in our area. Their team set up a huge tent outside the hospital for those who were infected and also used the women's ward for those with special needs, enabling them to isolate the cholera patients.

The epidemic taxed hospital resources to the maximum. Cholera Laboratory personnel were housed everywhere: in our homes, in the guesthouse, and in vacant missionary houses. They overflowed the hospital and drove up and down the hospital roads day and night as they went about their duties. Our small jungle hospital turned into a major medical facility overnight. Cholera Laboratory personnel gave the MCH staff hands-on training in communicable disease. Their first instruction was, "Wash your hands. If you wash your hands every time you touch a patient, you won't get cholera." I'm not sure any of us really believed them, but they were right. Not one of the MCH staff contracted cholera, despite continual, close contact with infected patients.

Because Bengalis use village ponds for everything from drinking, dishwashing, and bathing to laundry and washing the family cow, cholera spreads with incredible speed. It literally travels from pond to pond. People fleeing the infection in one place may pick it up somewhere down the road when they use an infected pond for their ablutions.

The cholera team at MCH so vigorously implemented a program of intravenous and oral fluid replacement that we lost few patients to the dread disease. If medical staff started treatment on them before they were completely dehydrated, adequate fluids pulled them back from the brink of death. It was a harrowing ordeal, but we were thankful for the Research Laboratory's help in winning the battle against the epidemic.

With the women's ward in use for cholera patients, we had even fewer beds for new patients, but that did not keep them from arriving in droves. Medical and surgical emergencies—unrelated to the cholera epidemic—still clamored for attention. The surgical schedule was full, and everyone worked overtime. It was difficult to keep sterile supplies on hand and adequate staff in the operating room. The giant puzzle became more complex every day.

One afternoon a tall, handsome Hindu gentleman was admitted for emergency surgery. Mr. Dhar was placed in the center aisle of the male ward on the only available bed. Mr. Dhar's petite wife, a small child in her arms and two others clinging to her sari, waited anxiously for her husband to come back from surgery. Her older children stayed at home; she had brought only the three youngest with her. When Vic Olsen operated on him, Mr. Dhar was found to have inoperable abdominal cancer. Although just forty-six years old, he had only a short time to live.

The day following Mr. Dhar's surgery was almost a repeat: a full surgery schedule. At noon, Donn Ketcham ran home for a bite of lunch while I circulated in the operating room. I was suddenly called out to see an emergency patient in OPD. I took one look at a pale, floppy baby, and sent a hurried message back to Donn's house, telling him to come quickly. Other staff members rushed to help me.

The tiny little girl, just ten months old and obviously well nourished, had long, silky eyelashes; a sweet, round face; and a rosebud mouth. At the moment I first saw her, she was turning blue from lack of oxygen. Her mother had been sitting on the floor cleaning fish, while the baby sat next to her and watched. Quick as a wink, the child popped a fish into her mouth and inhaled. The fish lodged firmly in her throat, shutting off her air supply. Her frantic father climbed on a bus and rode an agonizing twenty miles for help. As the baby fought desperately for air, the fish moved ever so slightly, allowing a tiny bit of air to enter her lungs. The baby was slowly suffocating.

I snatched the closest transfer forceps and with great difficulty grabbed most of the small, round fish. The baby took a deep breath and so did I. She could breathe now, but I was afraid she might inhale bits of fish still in the back of her throat. By the time I had pulled out most of the fish, Donn roared up on his motorcycle. Between surgical cases, he took the baby back to the OR and pulled the remaining pieces of fish out of her throat. We admitted her to the ward for observation but were confident she would be ready to go home the next day.

After we finished the last surgical case, I went into the ward to check on the baby before I left the hospital. Our little tyke was breathing heavily, but was not in any danger. Late that evening, Donn and Vic took her into the OR to examine her. Her throat had swollen, interfering with her breathing. The particular species of fish she swallowed has bristly, poisonous spines on its head. The spines had penetrated her throat and left their poison behind. While the doctors were working on her, the beautiful baby died.

For some reason I didn't get the news. The evening nurse didn't know the little girl had died, so that information was not included on her evening report. Because the night nurse thought I had received the information earlier, she did not include it on her night report. And because the baby's name did not appear on either report, I assumed her condition was stable.

Consequently, when a Bengali nurse greeted me the next morning with, "Sister, what shall I do with the body?" I was stunned. When Donn arrived a few minutes later, he explained what had happened. It was the beginning of a bad day.

When I made rounds with the doctors later that morning, we witnessed a pitiful scene at Mr. Dhar's bedside. Vic told the family about Mr. Dhar's inoperable cancer, and that he only had a few months to live. Now Mr. Dhar's family attempted to cope with the fact that there was nothing that would help him. The waste of precious lives seemed senseless and hopelessly sad.

Early in my nurse's training, I learned to control my emotions. I received my R.N. degree in 1955, at a time when it was considered unacceptable for a nurse to speak loudly on the wards, let alone weep or faint, even in a dire emergency. No matter what happened, a nurse's iron control must never slip. But that day at MCH, I fell apart. I barely managed to keep my composure until I reached my room. I cried for the dead baby, for Mr. Dhar, for the cholera patients. Probably, I cried most of all from sheer exhaustion. I could not stop crying, no matter how hard I tried. My director of nurses from Highland Hospital certainly would have questioned my emotional stability that day! It took hours for my tears to stop and my topsy-turvy world to right itself.

By the weekend, things had quieted down. The wards were still badly overloaded, but at least no new emergencies arose. On Sunday when I went into the hospital to make afternoon rounds, the Holy Spirit spoke very clearly to my heart. "Go and talk to the Dhar family about the love of Jesus, and I will help them understand."

With a Bengali Gospel of John in my hand, I sat down by Mr. Dhar's bed. Mr. and Mrs. Dhar listened carefully as I spoke. I talked to them about how much God loved them and explained that Jesus Christ had given His life for their sins. I shared my own testimony of finding Christ as a child and about all He had done for me. As we talked, I knew their hearts were prepared. They asked searching, intelligent questions. I spoke of the impossibility of finding peace with God through our own good works or through animal sacrifice. Then I prayed with them and asked them to consider accepting Jesus Christ as personal Savior. They promised to think about it.

Monday was another busy day. As I was preparing 8 a.m. medications, wondering how we would ever finish all the work scheduled for the day, Vic Olsen began morning rounds alone. He soon left the ward to find me. "That Hindu family wants to accept Christ right now," he said. "I want you to go and talk to them." I knew it would be a long time before I could get to Mr. Dhar's bedside. Some chores in a hospital must be done on time, and giving out medications is one of them!

When things quieted down, I went back to talk to Mr. and Mrs. Dhar. Vic was right. They were both ready to accept Christ, and it gave me much joy to lead them to the Savior. What a comfort it was to know that Mr. Dhar would go to heaven when he died.

A few days later, we sent the family home to their Hindu village, Satan's territory. I knew the Holy Spirit would keep Mr. Dhar safe until God took him to heaven. Mr. Dhar was confined to his bed, but reading his Bengali Bible gave him strength in those difficult days. He was an active witness to his Hindu neighbors to the end of his earthly life.

In all these difficult situations and many more, God was our strength, giving us opportunities to grow in grace and enabling us to reach out to sick and grieving nationals around us.

fourteen

Creepy Crawlies

Bangladesh has its share of creepy crawlies. Most of them are harmless; some are ugly enough to be frightening; many have merely nuisance value. The ones I saw most often were cockroaches, lizards, spiders, and snakes. Sometimes the creatures that we couldn't see did the most damage. I was susceptible to malaria and usually didn't see the evil bearers of that disease until it was too late.

White ants (termites) do a great deal of hidden damage. One tiny flaw in a cement floor can let a flood of these invaders into a house. White ants can start on the bottom shelf of a bookcase and eat their way through an entire library, without any sign of forced entry. White ants eat their way through wood and books, gluing everything together with sticky mud trails full of larvae.

Bengalis store their good clothes and valuable papers in metal trunks and boxes redolent of mothballs. We learned to store our good clothes, books, and valuables in metal drums. However, we found that unless a metal drum was tightly sealed, it could not keep out the voracious white ant. If you left even the tiniest opening, they'd come swarming in and devour everything you had carefully packed for future use!

Never having lived in the tropics before, I was shocked by the size of the cockroaches. The variety we saw most often is officially known as "the great Texas cockroach." Houses are wide open most of the year, so these ugly creatures wander in and out freely, clambering under doors, through holes in screens, or into uncovered air vents.

Cockroaches are intimidating because they whiz drunkenly through the air, and it's anybody's guess where they will land—perhaps in your hair, down your neck, or up your pant leg. Turn on the kitchen light and a horde of the wretched creatures scurries in every direction to get out of the light. After you've gone to bed, you may be awakened in the middle of the night by a loud *crunch, crunch*. It's probably a cockroach, feasting on scrap paper in the wastebasket. Now you face a major dilemma. Should you get up in the dark and finish him off? If you turn on the light, he will vanish into thin air. If you don't turn on the light, you may step on something far worse than a cockroach. It's probably best to put your pillow over your head to muffle the noise. Perhaps you will drift off to sleep and dream . . . of giant cockroaches climbing inside your mosquito net.

Newcomers to Bangladesh always made us chuckle when they met their first really big cockroach. Cockroaches move quickly, and we learned to kill them with one blow from a sandal. If the first blow misses, you seldom get a second chance. But it takes awhile for a newcomer to get used to the drill. The usual first response is to raise your legs as high as possible to keep the creature from crawling up your pants or trailing skirt. While we mounted continual forays against these pests, we realized that winning the battle was a far cry from winning the war.

Our experiences with a common pest, the housefly, sometimes led to awkward situations. The year before the hospital opened, our field council arranged an Islamic Conference for our missionaries, with Miss Irene West, of London, England, as guest lecturer. A charming British woman, she had extensive missionary experience among Muslims. We enjoyed listening to her lectures, as well as chatting with her between sessions.

One evening, as a group of us sat at the dining room table drinking coffee and eating dessert, a fly settled dangerously close to the luscious cake on the table. With one quick move of his hand, a missionary colleague snatched the fly and expertly flipped it—

into Irene West's coffee! We all responded with laughter at his expense, of course. Miss West was a good sport and laughed with the rest of us, but the poor missionary turned beet red. In fact, if we brought up the subject of Miss West and the fly today, I'm sure we'd get the same response—loud laughter and a red-faced missionary.

Flies in dessert occurred on more than one occasion in Chittagong. I remember the day Jay and El Walsh entertained company from the U.S. El's magnificent lemon meringue pie held the place of honor on the luncheon table. Out of nowhere, a roving fly landed in the middle of El's perfect meringue. Jay was the one most upset, but it didn't really matter. The young, svelte guest was watching her figure and didn't eat pie anyhow. One fly, pulled off of the pie discreetly, didn't bother Jay or the rest of us; we enjoyed the delicious dessert with gratitude for the occasion that prompted El to make it.

I'm not afraid of spiders, but some people find them petrifying. These creatures often rest on bathroom or bedroom walls, probably waiting for dinner to wander by. Some are large and hairy, with glittering eyes. Trying to kill them poses a problem. You have to plan your strategy. What weapon do you have? Will your sandal reach the creature, or will it send him scurrying for cover or down on your head? The situation may be compounded if it's a mama spider carrying her progeny in a huge sac attached to her tummy. If the first blow doesn't kill her, you may scatter a new generation of spiders all over the room.

Some of the lizards in Bangladesh are heard but not seen. Many creatures are known to Bengalis by the word that describes the sound they make. A frog really does say *beng, beng,* so a frog is called a beng. If you ask someone who has lived in Chittagong or Malumghat what goes *tik, tik, tik,* he will know immediately that you are talking about a gecko known as a *tik-tiki.* These little gray-green house lizards eat insects. Their tiny feet are equipped with suction pads that enable them to climb walls and perch on ceilings. Sometimes, though, they land with a *plop* on a table, a desk, an unsuspecting head, or even in the gravy boat.

House lizards are harmless little creatures, used to being around people. I once walked into a bathroom and reached for a cloth hung over a wall peg. Much to my surprise, I found a tiny gecko sound asleep, snuggled between two cloths hung on the peg to dry. He looked as though he had climbed into bed and pulled up the covers, ready for a long nap.

A much larger lizard, called a *tork-teng,* gets his name from the sound of his repeated call, resounding loudly throughout the house or verandah. His voice gets slower and slower, as though someone wound him up and his spring is gradually unwinding. He rarely ventures into society, but it is not uncommon to spot his silhouette on a verandah screen at night. He is gray-green, with bright red spots that make him look ferocious. The *tork-teng* usually stays out of sight unless disturbed or threatened.

Snakes were my nemesis! I'm happy to say that I encountered very few snakes, but each encounter reinforced my fear. Missionaries at Hebron had frequent snake encounters because of the surrounding jungle. When we lived at Hebron we always carried flashlights or lanterns at night. Our houses were far apart, with no outside lights to illuminate the grass. Snakes were a problem at Hebron during the hot and rainy seasons. In the winter, when the weather got really chilly at night, the snakes disappeared from sight until spring.

While Jay and El Walsh lived at Hebron, Jay built me a house on stilts. I felt quite secure; I couldn't imagine a snake getting into a house on stilts. Ha! One day my helper, Khoka, went into my house to move a heavy trunk while I worked out in the yard. I heard him yell, and he appeared at the front door calling, "Come over here! I want to show you something." Khoka exited the house with a huge snake slung over a big stick. The snake had been curled up behind the trunk and Khoka disturbed it when he moved the trunk away from the wall. He grabbed a big stick and killed the snake before it could strike him.

My house had woven bamboo walls and a metal roof. The walls of the verandah were made of graceful bamboo latticework. My companion at that time was a gangling Alsatian puppy named Jimmy. One morning when I went to the verandah door to let Jimmy out, I pushed open the lattice door and froze in shock. As the dog slipped out, I quietly pulled the door shut and retreated inside the house. Woven into the latticework beside the door was a slender, brilliant green snake. Sound asleep, it was almost invisible against the jungle greenery. When I heard Jabbar, the cook, crossing the lawn, I called him and told him to wait outside. I walked onto the verandah and pointed at the sleeping snake. Jabbar gasped and said, "*Oh, Ma-ray* (Oh, my Mother!), that snake is deadly poison!" Grabbing a stick, he struck the snake so hard it fell to the ground, where he quickly killed it. I could not believe how close I had come to putting my hand on the snake when I opened the door.

One evening Benu, the language teacher, walked with me to my house after prayer meeting at Jay and El's. We both carried flashlights as we strolled along, discussing the day's events. Suddenly, a snake slithered at high speed toward us. It was a brightly colored banded krait, one of the few poisonous snakes in Bangladesh. It climbed one side of a bamboo fence, slithered down the other side, and headed straight for us. Benu dropped his flashlight, grabbed a large stick, and began beating the snake. His severe fright gave him enough adrenaline to beat it to a pulp. I was immobilized with fear myself, and I was glad I wasn't walking the trail alone that night.

When ABWE built the mission hospital at Malumghat, some very large snakes were displaced from the nearby jungle. Tom McDonald, who supervised the building project, was an excellent marksman. One evening at dusk, when Tom walked through the living room of the nurse's residence, a movement behind a large chair caught his eye. Tom sprinted for his rifle, took careful aim, and killed the biggest krait I have ever seen.

Another afternoon at the nurse's residence, I sat in my room typing a prayer letter. I was writing about problems we faced at the hospital, attributing them to Satan. I got up for a minute to stretch and then walked out onto the verandah. Much to my amazement, a huge, muddy gray serpent slithered straight down the middle of the front lawn. His head was raised high, showing his bright, intelligent eyes. He looked almost friendly. I watched for a few minutes, then made a move that alerted the snake to my presence. It quickly slid over the edge of the riverbank and vanished from view. I'm sure it was just a big water snake enjoying a tour of the compound. The snake was no threat to my safety right then, but it definitely brought to life my words about the wiles of the Devil.

The most frightening encounter I had with a snake at Malumghat occurred when Becky and I shared an apartment in the Bengali nurse's residence. The apartment windows were well-screened to keep mosquitoes, lizards, and all other forms of reptilia outside. One afternoon I got off my bed after siesta and pushed aside the frilly white curtains to let in a little air. As I put my hand on the curtain, something slid under my hand and fell to the floor with a thump. I jumped into the middle of my bed screaming "Snake, Snake!" at the top of my lungs.

Poor Becky was rudely awakened. Her quiet voice calmed me. "Where are you?" she asked from her bedroom.

"On my bed," I replied shakily.

"Where's the snake? Can you see it?"

"Yes, it's in the corner by the bookcase."

"Stay where you are and keep your eye on it. I'll run and get the *darwan* (guard)."

I heard Becky run down the road toward the hospital. Soon she was back with the *darwan,* his heavy baton in hand. He looked calm and confident, both of which I definitely was not! The *darwan* looked at the snake through the screen door, then walked into my room and around the bed. One blow of his baton dispatched the snake. He flung it over his stick and went off to show the other *darwans* the evidence of his valor.

Becky and I were relieved that the snake was dead. I was thankful the snake had stayed put until the guard arrived. Nothing would have moved me off my bed with a snake loose in the house.

Creepy crawlies: Some are fun to watch; most are harmless and innocent; some we do our best to exterminate; and a few we try to avoid at all cost. All are part of the scenery and add interest to the tropical paradise that is Bangladesh.

fifteen

Speaking of Angels

While we were certainly aware of satanic oppression, we also knew that God sometimes protected us in unusual ways, particularly when we faced danger. God probably also intervened in our lives even when we didn't know we needed His help.

Malumghat lies only sixty-seven miles south of Chittagong, but the road between the two locations can be formidable. In recent years, the road has been widened to two lanes. For many years, however, it was a narrow lane-and-a-half for two-way traffic. The original road is World War II vintage, built to provide access to Allied air bases in Chittagong and Cox's Bazar. The road snakes through acre after acre of rice paddies and between village *bazars* swarming with people. Its tiny one-lane bridges span innumerable rivers and streams. There are so many blind curves and corners that it's a wise driver who keeps his hand on the horn. The government patches the road every cool season, gluing it together with brick chips and liquid tar.

While freezing temperatures in North America make roads buckle and heave, torrential rains and floods in the tropics leave roads full of huge potholes, cracks, and eroded shoulders after every rainy season. Tons of goods shipped from Chittagong to markets all the way south to Cox's Bazar travel the road in overloaded trucks. This enormous volume of heavy traffic causes additional road damage.

The unwritten rule of the country is that a smaller vehicle gives way to a larger vehicle. Thus, a car or van, when facing an oncoming bus or truck, creeps over to the shoulder (when there is one, that is). Bengali drivers seem to enjoy playing "chicken." If one wants to face down an opposing vehicle and can do so without succumbing to a heart attack, he will hold his ground. The driver *might* veer at the last possible moment, leaving the non-mover the victor in the contest. Most of us, however, decided that the risks were not worth the potential trauma. We preferred to back down and give way to the vehicle rushing toward us.

God has been gracious to those of us who traveled that road for decades. We all have horror stories about our trips to and from Malumghat. Our tales include everything from bandits and elephants to flat tires, teetering rickshaws, and boiling radiators. All of us have been very much aware of God's hand on us and our vehicles.

I don't like to drive, and I never felt completely at ease driving between Chittagong and Malumghat. The grueling trip was not much fun for me or my passenger. MCH now owns several vehicles and employs drivers who traverse the route regularly and know every blind curve and pothole. They actually seem to enjoy the trip, and an experienced driver makes the trip more pleasant for everyone.

I remember a day when some nurses traveled to Chittagong with colleague Jane Golin. We were about halfway there when a truck tried to get around Jane's van. Both vehicles had slowed to a crawl because of road construction. I sat in the front right-hand seat, next to the door. In Bangladesh, all vehicles drive on the left and the passing lane is on the right, so the truck was passing on my side. Just as it drew alongside, the truck tipped in our direction. The truck body hit our right wing window, breaking it into thousands of glass pellets. No one was hurt, but our laps were full of glass. When Jane could pull off the road safely, she stopped the van so we could climb out and shake the glass from our clothing. It was merely an inconvenience, nothing more. We climbed back in the van and went on our way.

Just a few miles down the road, a bus was hurtling toward us when we heard a loud bang. The bus began swerving sideways, headed straight for our van. We could see the driver struggling to regain control of his vehicle. Jane prayed, "Oh, God, please keep it away from us." We watched in horrified fascination as the bus drew closer, before skidding to a stop. A few minutes made all the difference in the world. I have often recalled how a minor incident delayed us for a few minutes and prevented a potentially fatal accident. God had everything under control.

After East Pakistan's War of Independence in 1971, I became deeply involved in a women's rehabilitation ministry. All of the supplies for this ministry came from Chittagong's large wholesale market. It was fun traveling to town for a day or two, and I enjoyed the challenge of hunting down the items I needed for my work. Malumghat missionaries always liked to visit the Chittagong missionaries and eat out in a Chinese restaurant or the large air-conditioned hotel.

On one of my regular trips to Chittagong, Linda Short was my traveling companion when I was driving a Volkswagen bug. The ravages of war had left the road in bad shape, and several bridges were out. What we call detours in America are called "diversions" in Bangladesh. That is probably an excellent name for them; they are diverting in the extreme! There were several diversions I had to negotiate with extreme caution. Linda and I were relieved when we finally arrived in Chittagong—hot, sticky, and tired, but safe.

After a long day in the busy wholesale market, we finished our list of errands. We stayed overnight at the ABWE Guest House, and early the next morning headed for Malumghat in our little car. Although fun, Chittagong also was hot and noisy, and we were eager to return to Malumghat's relative quiet and cooler temperatures.

Because of the deplorable driving conditions, I had to give my full attention to the road in front of us. Road hazards are different from those found in America. In Bangladesh, motorists have to dodge cows, goats, chickens, dogs, roadside markets, and coolies carrying heavy loads. There are also potholes, missing pavement, drying rice straw, buses, trucks, autos, and absent road signs.

We were making good time when something happened. Linda had just leaned under the dashboard to retrieve something from her tote bag when I heard a voice clearly and urgently say, "Put on your brakes. There's no road."

I slammed on my brakes and screeched to a stop within a few feet of a 40-foot drop to a dry riverbed. The bridge was out. Usually a pile of bricks or stones in the middle of the road is the sign of a missing bridge, but there was absolutely nothing to warn of the hazard.

Linda came up from beneath the dash, sputtering, "What are you doing? Why did you slam on your brakes like that?" She looked through the windshield and gasped. We sat there and shook. Our heavily loaded VW, dropping from the jagged pavement to the rocky riverbed below, might well have brought our missionary careers to an abrupt end.

A guardian angel stood in our path, spoke a clear warning, and we were spared. We thanked God profusely for His timely intervention in our lives. I drove the rest of the way home with extreme caution.

There it was—the first fence, the first hospital building, the teeming, bustling roadside *bazar*—Malumghat. "*Thank you*, Lord, for sending your angel to guard us today. *Thank you* for bringing us safely home."

sixteen

Called to Help

Missionary kids (MKs) have always been the missionaries' best cheerleaders, encouragers, and prayer warriors. We always said that if you really needed a prayer answered, you had better ask the kids to pray. They had a great deal of faith and expected God to hear and answer their prayers immediately, if not sooner. They were lots of fun, too, helping the adults keep their sanity when life seemed overwhelming. Work, especially in the hospital, took great chunks of time and stamina. We adults drooped in the hot season and steamed in the monsoons. But the MKs could be covered with prickly heat or boils and still race around the soccer field as if it were a cool, fall day in Pennsylvania. They were amazing!

We adults picked up nicknames, partly because we lived so closely together on the compound, and partly because we felt like family. The extended family included missionary "aunts" and "uncles." I think some missionary kids were not quite sure which family was their own. They were used to walking into Aunt Marge's house for a cookie, or helping Uncle Bob start the generator. Anyhow, in their eyes we were all part of the family. One little tyke even called her father "Uncle Daddy." Talk about confusion!

I had a bad year early in my nursing career at Malumghat. The hospital was so short-staffed, it seemed as though the few of us there were always on duty. Dr. Donn Ketcham handled the ever-expanding patient load by himself; nurse Jean Weld supervised the outpatient department and helped in surgery, while I supervised medical/surgical patients, the central supply room, and the operating room. We were just starting to train Bengali assistants, so the three of us still carried many responsibilities in all departments.

Even after working all day at the hospital, we were often called out at night for emergency surgery. I remember one night in particular when we scheduled emergency surgery. The generator that provided lights for the operating room wasn't working. Donn Ketcham sat on the floor of the "genny" shack, patiently laid out the parts, made the necessary repairs, and reassembled the generator. That was his *first* operation of the evening. Two more operations—on people—were to follow. I used to tell him he was the only surgeon I knew who smelled of diesel fuel.

The one bright spot in that year was a little MK named David Ketcham, who could not have been more than three years old at the time. I walked home from the hospital every night at dusk, bone weary and often ready to throw in the towel. There on a corner stood a sturdy little boy, patiently awaiting my arrival. He never said more than two words, and they were always the same: "Hi, Louly!" That was David's name for me. And now, many years later, I still hear it from my colleagues or see it written in a letter. He was the star on my horizon, and I'm not sure I would have made it through the year without him.

One year I came back from furlough with a brand-new Schwinn, adult, three-wheeled tricycle. I thought it would be a big help getting to and from the hospital. Three-wheelers take considerable energy, but they are good exercise. Riding the trike also got me where I was going a lot faster than walking.

The older boys loved to tease me about it. "Aunt Mary Lou," Phil Walsh would jest, "when are you going to take the training wheels off that thing?"

Or Dan DeCook would ask, "When are you going to ride that thing to the hospital?"

I had a problem, and I'm sure the boys knew it. There is just one hill between the housing area and the hospital. It isn't an especially *big* hill, but it looked like a mountain to me. It scared me to death. I just could not bring myself to ride down it, something I had to do if I wanted to ride to the hospital. Talk about being chicken *numero uno*—I was it.

One day after kid's choir practice at the Guest House, Steve DeCook hopped on his bike and pulled along the right side of my three-wheeler. "Steve," I asked grumpily, "just what do you think you're doing?"

He flashed me his biggest smile and said, "I'm going to help you get down that hill."

I said sarcastically, "Are you going to pick up the pieces when I break my neck, too?"

"Oh, Aunt Mary Lou," he said, "of course I would. But you aren't going to fall. Look, just put your foot on the pedal, push back on it and give it a little brake. Then ride straight down the middle of the hill. You'll be surprised how easy it is. Don't be afraid. I'm right here beside you." We rode straight down the hill together and, much to my surprise, that big mountain turned into a small hill.

I have thought of that moment so many times since then, especially when God has provided a helper in answer to a fervent prayer. We never would have survived at Malumghat without the help of many people. Some scheduled their arrival months or years ahead, while others just dropped in unexpectedly.

For example, at the time I was trying to organize the pharmacy warehouse, everyone else was too busy to help me sort the building full of medicines and hospital supplies. Before I could unpack boxes and stock drugs, I first needed sturdy shelves, which someone would have to design and build. Besides, there were invoices to check and a host of other details to handle.

I prayed, *"Lord, I just can't do this. There are too many demands on my time now. I really can't take on any more responsibility. If I have to do it, it's not going to get done—maybe not ever."* God already knew that and had picked the right person for the job. Out of the blue walked a red-haired, freckle-faced young man. Jerry Flaming was traveling around the world, stopping at mission stations and lending a hand to anyone who needed help, and he became an instant friend. He loved the missionary community, related well to our MKs, and proved to be a willing, capable worker.

Tackling the drug storage problem, he crafted metal frames in our workshop, set them up in the warehouse, and fitted them with wooden shelves. Jerry cheerfully unpacked boxes and stocked shelves in a tin-roofed warehouse. He worked in heat that produces eye-blinding, shirt-soaking, nose-dripping sweat. After several weeks of hard work, he finished the job and moved on. When we asked why he had to leave, Jerry put it succinctly: "If I stay here any longer, I'll be here forever."

A steady stream of doctors, nurses, dentists, physical therapists, office managers, teachers, and other helpers often kept the medical work afloat during periods of serious personnel shortage. They will never know what their presence meant to weary, overburdened missionaries.

The Holy Spirit is our Helper, "called alongside" to encourage and walk with us through our day-by-day experiences. He sometimes illustrates the reality of His presence by sending special helpers for our encouragement at the very moment that we need them most.

s e v e n t e e n

Cyclone!

What is the correct word for a tropical storm? Is it a cyclone, a hurricane, or a typhoon? When I was on deputation, someone asked me what kind of tropical storms we had in Bangladesh—were they tornadoes or hurricanes? I was momentarily confused, since neither word is used in Bangladesh. We finally resolved the issue when I told him that our storms inevitably form over water, rather than over land. That obviously made them hurricanes. Bengalis use the interesting word *toophon,* probably a twist on the word typhoon. The most common word for the vicious storms that frequently devastate Bangladesh is "cyclone." Bangladesh has a long coastline that stretches from the north side of the Bay of Bengal south to Burma. Cyclones wreak havoc on the country, destroying homes, cattle, and crops, and sometimes separating families forever.

Before I lived in East Pakistan I never witnessed anything worse than a bad snowstorm. Where I grew up in western New York we didn't have tornadoes, so I was totally unprepared for the violence of the storms that ravage Bangladesh year after year.

Hebron caught the tail end of a cyclone when I lived there my first term in a small bamboo house sheltered by a hill. During the monsoon season, wind often blew rain through the bamboo latticework into my house. On this occasion, however, the sky grew quite dark even though it was only dusk. I saw just a spattering of rain, no thunder or lightning. Every time I lit my kerosene lantern, the wind blew it out. I finally gave up, tucked my mosquito net firmly under my mattress, and climbed into bed. When I woke up early the next morning, the storm had passed and the sky was clear and blue.

Jay Walsh had gone to Chittagong to buy food supplies. When he returned to Hebron, he said, "Mary Lou, you won't recognize Chittagong when you see it. A terrible storm stripped off leaves and foliage at third-floor level. Huge trees toppled over. I've never seen destruction like that before."

I couldn't imagine such a scene in Chittagong, always so lush and green; but when I visited the city a few weeks later, I understood what Jay meant. The trees still standing had lost all their leaves and branches at third-floor level, just as he said. In the government guesthouse yard, many trees lay overturned, with their roots exposed. Smaller trees looked as though they had been scorched by fire.

My first experience of a cyclone took place in Chittagong in 1960, when one struck without warning. I was staying alone at the mission Guest House, planning to fly to Dacca the next morning to renew my passport. I awoke in the middle of the night to the sound of banging windows. I slipped on my sandals and walked into the living room, where several windows swung back and forth. I fastened as many as I could, but several with warped frames would not shut. Glass shattered as the windows swung in the wind, and the floor was soon littered with shards of glass and puddles of rainwater, blown in by the raging wind.

I felt like one of the foolish virgins in Matthew 25. I found a kerosene lantern, but it was out of oil. But that didn't really matter, because I couldn't find matches either. Chittagong Medical College occupied the hill opposite the Guest House, and its lights shone out of the darkness. The light silhouetted palm trees bent almost double in the wind. Torrential rain soaked everything. I was in a sturdy building—safe, warm, and dry—but those who lived in bamboo houses must have been wet, uncomfortable, and frightened. Even a moderate cyclone has the power to destroy fragile bamboo houses—and everything in them.

It was impossible to fly to Dacca the next morning. Airport runways were flooded, and I had to reschedule my trip to the American Embassy. That was as close to a cyclone as I ever wanted to get.

For many years, Bangladesh did not have the necessary technology to predict cyclones. Once it obtained the technology and equipment, the government faced the challenge of getting the news to the affected area *before* a cyclone struck. During a cyclone, storm-churned waters sometimes sweep completely over an island, dislodging everything in the way. For several years, the government built dikes around vulnerable areas, such as islands. Dikes built higher than any known tidal wave appeared to solve the problem, until an enormous tidal wave swept over the dike on one island, submerging everything trapped inside the dike. I still remember the newspaper article that listed relief goods needed on the island. The writer ended by saying, "Please don't send any children's clothing. There are no children left on the island."

After that, the government began building multipurpose community centers, specially designed as storm centers. These buildings dot the landscape between Memorial Christian Hospital and Cox's Bazar. They are visible from a long distance because they are built on concrete posts, high above the reach of tidal waves. These sturdy buildings offer the best chance of survival in a major storm.

There is still one small problem, though. Bengalis often refuse to leave their homes in times of danger. Their reasoning is no different than that of an American who refuses to leave the Outer Banks when a hurricane threatens, or a man who insists on staying at his house even though a forest fire is raging nearby, so he can hose down the roof. They may lose their lives, but they must protect their property. Bamboo and mud houses cannot withstand shrieking winds and rising floodwaters, and many Bengalis lose their lives trying to hang on to their few meager possessions.

When I worked at Memorial Christian Hospital, I met a young man who had survived a devastating cyclone. Listening to his story gave me a much better idea of the anguish Bengalis suffer when they face these terrible storms.

Sanjib Boidya was born in Barisal district, a delta area on the north side of the Bay of Bengal. He grew up in a nominal Christian home in a small village. Itinerant British Baptist missionaries had evangelized his Hindu village many years earlier.

Sanjib's family lived on an alluvial plain dotted by small islands called *jhils*. The *jhils* barely rise above the water at high tide, but the land is fertile because of the silt left behind at the end of the rainy season. Sanjib laughingly recalls the time he was secretary of his church's Ladies Missionary Society. "I was able to row a boat," he says. "That was the one requirement for the job, so they gave it to me. I used to row the boat from house to house, picking the ladies up for their meetings and taking them home again."

People live peacefully on these small islands until a cyclone strikes. Then there is no way out, and the loss of life is phenomenal. When Sanjib tells the story of that fateful night, he makes it sound as though it happened yesterday.

Sanjib's story began on a gloomy evening in May, just a few weeks before the monsoon rains, which usually start in June. He says, "This particular night, people were nervous because the wind kept shifting. We had no official warning in the village but, by midnight, we knew a violent storm was brewing. I was staying at my sister's house because her husband was away and she was afraid to stay alone with her three children. We both got up several times to check on the rising water and reassure the children. The roar of the wind was so loud, the children cried in fear. We two adults tried to remain calm, even though we knew there was no high ground on the island. No matter what happened, we had no other place to go."

Almost without warning, water reached the front step of

Sanjib's sister's house. Moments later, wind blew away the tiny bamboo house's verandah. The roof and walls went next. Only one center post remained. The water rose rapidly to waist height. Sanjib, his sister, and the two boys grasped the pole tightly. Sanjib held his infant niece in his arms, struggling to keep her above the water. Repeatedly, over the roar of the storm, his sister pleaded with him to let the baby go. "If you hold her any longer, you'll both be swept away. Let her go. Let her go."

But Sanjib held the baby tightly in his arms. "If she dies, we'll die together," he screamed above the howling wind. "I can't let her go."

Finally, in a moment of quiet, Sanjib's sister grabbed a nearby tree. Now Sanjib and the boys had a little more room and it was easier for him to firmly grip the post. Somehow, they held on until dawn. Suddenly, the water began to recede, taking scores of cattle, houses, and villagers out to sea. But Sanjib and his sister's family refused to let go. "The water felt as though someone heated it," he says. "Otherwise, we probably would have died of exposure. God spared my life, even though I didn't really know Him then."

The seawater, warmed by the sun, spread over the land, filling it like a giant bathtub. When the water receded, it was as though someone pulled the plug and let all the water out. People, food, clothing, household goods, and houses vanished. The receding sea covered the land with slimy mud, ruining crops and contaminating drinking water.

Sanjib and his sister began a frantic search for the rest of their family. Their mother, father, brothers, and baby sister had sheltered together in a small house nearby. Sanjib continues, "We found my father and two of my brothers buried to their waists in mud. They had no clothing, but they were alive! I found a muddy curtain and a pair of trousers for them while we continued to search for my mother. We looked everywhere, but couldn't find her."

Sanjib's mother, baby sister, and three little brothers perished in the storm. His weeping father told Sanjib what happened. "We tied the little boys together. We thought we could hang onto them that way, but the wind and tide were too strong. We couldn't save them. At least they were together. They didn't have to die alone."

Heartsick and almost insane with grief, the decimated family tried to find a way to survive. Sanjib recalls, "There was no food or water until relief teams arrived a week later. We ate banana stalks, which were moist and nourishing. We gleaned rice in salty fields. We couldn't build fires because everything was soaked. Somehow, we stayed alive until help came."

When the raging sea finally calmed, relief teams brought food, fresh water, and clothing. They also brought in bamboo and helped villagers rebuild their homes. But how do you rebuild families torn apart by devastating loss?

Sanjib's wise father knew that the village economy could no longer support his family. He pled with Sanjib, "You're a high school graduate. We're depending on you. Do something to help your family. Go to school, learn a trade, or find a job in Dacca. We'll all have to work hard to rebuild our family and village."

But Sanjib, swamped with grief, had little heart for anything. A friend, hearing of Sanjib's loss, made a special trip to see him. "Sanjib," he said, "why don't you study nursing at a Christian hospital? Just think of all the good you could do in your village if you took nurse's training. I work at a mission hospital in Chandraghona. That's not too far from here. I think you'd like it there." But Sanjib refused to commit himself.

His friend returned to Chandraghona and told the nursing supervisor about his troubled friend. She immediately wrote a letter inviting Sanjib to join the next nursing class. But Sanjib still wasn't sure about nursing. He sent a letter of refusal. The superintendent, sensing his desperation, repeated the invitation. This time Sanjib decided to try; he left for Chandraghona.

Four years of intense training followed. "The course was only three-and-a-half years," Sanjib admits, "but I flunked anatomy by one point and had to repeat the class." The discipline and training helped restore Sanjib's emotional balance.

While at Chandraghona, he met a petite young lady, a distant cousin. He had met her briefly in Barisal, where she tutored in village homes. Now she, too, was training to become a nurse. Classmates encouraged their betrothal. After their marriage, Sanjib and his bride worked in several mission hospitals.

"Something was missing," he says. "I didn't know what it was, but it left me dissatisfied with my life. I love nursing, but I wanted to learn more about God and I couldn't seem to do that, even in Christian hospitals."

During this time of searching, a former classmate wrote to Sanjib and said, "If you want to preach and serve God, come to Memorial Christian Hospital. There are plenty of opportunities for Christian service, and the staff is encouraged to study the Bible, to preach, and to witness." This sounded like Sanjib's idea of a *real* mission hospital. He made arrangements for an interview and was appointed as a staff nurse.

Dr. Vic Olsen and Jesse Eaton, the hospital administrator, immediately began to talk to Sanjib about Christ. Day after day they discussed Bible verses with him, encouraging Sanjib to study God's Word for himself. One day, when Sanjib invited the doctor to have tea at his house, Vic carefully reviewed the plan of salvation with him. Finally, he asked, "Sanjib, don't you and your wife want to accept Jesus Christ as Savior? You can do it right now if you wish." Sanjib and his wife did just that.

"It was a wonderful day," Sanjib says. "I have never been so happy in my whole life. My wife and I bubbled over with joy in Christ." And that joy has remained. Milli, their oldest daughter, is a bright child. Sweeti, their youngest, is brain damaged and has cerebral palsy. But Sanjib and his wife have found Christ faithful even in trial and heartache. "Perhaps," he muses, "if it hadn't been for the cyclone, I never would have come to Christ." God's way, though sometimes hard, is always best.

eighteen

How War Happened

One of the most difficult times we faced in East Pakistan was the War of Independence, fought from March to December of 1971, resulting in the creation of Bangladesh. I think all of us who lived through that time still find the war hard to describe. Was it a civil war? Yes, it was. Was it a revolution? Yes, it was that, too. Did East Pakistan secede from West Pakistan? Yes, she most certainly did. Did the war involve genocide? Yes, of the most inhuman kind. How did the war come about?

Until Bangladesh declared independence, the country had been East Pakistan, provincial stepsister of West Pakistan. East Pakistan was carved out of India's East Bengal province in 1947, when Mohammed Jinnah and the Muslims in India agitated for a nation of their own. At the same time, India was gaining its independence from English colonial rule. As all men who carve out new nations have discovered, this was a difficult proposition. The idolatry of the Hindus sorely tried the patience of the monotheistic Muslims. Nor were the Hindus great lovers of Islam. The two factions often clashed violently, particularly on religious holidays.

After much negotiation, cartographers in England created a new nation out of India. Because there were large enclaves of Muslims in two widely separated areas of the subcontinent, the new country had two wings, East and West Pakistan. West Pakistan, a rugged, mountainous area on the western side of India, with progressive cities and a healthy infrastructure, became the center of commerce and government. Underdeveloped East Pakistan, a tiny, rain-drenched alluvial plain on the east side of India, became more like a province. She had no military, and was administered by a resident governor. Her road system was in poor repair; her railway hopelessly antiquated. She had to move most commercial goods by boat. West Pakistan boasted an excellent road and railway system, which simplified commerce considerably.

When the nations' borders were drawn, East Pakistan's jute, representing a large share of the commercial livelihood, remained in the country. The mills that processed the jute, however, remained in India. Chittagong Port belonged to East Pakistan, but it contained no machinery with which to load and unload the large ships entering its harbor. At the time of India's partition, Chittagong was a small, untidy town situated at the mouth of the Karnafuli River. East Pakistan had to build a viable port facility with little more than hacksaws because she had none of the sophisticated machinery found in industrialized countries.

A great deal of blood stained the ground on both sides of the Indian border in 1947. Muslims pushed Hindus back into India, and Hindus shoved Muslims into Pakistan, both sides hacking and burning as they ran. Families were divided and businesses abandoned as the tide of religious rage swept the subcontinent.

West Pakistan is a nation of tall, vigorous wheat-eaters, used to frigid winters and rugged mountains. Its people are fierce, sturdy warriors; their heritage includes Alexander the Great and Genghis Khan. They are muscular and fair-skinned; some have blue or hazel eyes. Their women are statuesque, sturdy, and strong. Urdu and Pushto are the common languages, although mountain tribes speak their own dialects. Many of these people are nomadic, herding goats or sheep during the summer months and retreating to lower altitudes before winter snows block the mountain passes.

By contrast, the Bengalis of East Pakistan are petite and brown-skinned, with dark eyes and hair as black as a raven's wing. They are volatile, artistic, poetic, and romantic. Most are, of necessity, farmers. Their heart's desire is to pass on their family's land to the next generation, even if it is a tiny rice paddy almost too small to farm. Bengalis are used to a hot climate and even hotter food. They like their curry redolent with chili peppers. In personality, language, and customs, they are as different from the West Pakistanis as day is from night. Only one bond could hold this diverse nation together: the religion called Islam. Was that tenuous bond enough to weld these widely disparate people?

As if this were not enough, 1,000 miles of unfriendly India separated East and West Pakistan. Entrepreneurs shipped raw materials from East Pakistan's fields and jungles to ports in East Pakistan, then around India by sea to West Pakistan. The goods were then processed in West Pakistani factories, shipped back to East Pakistan, and sold in shops and markets. Many of those involved in this lucrative business venture were wealthy West Pakistanis living in East Pakistan.

East Pakistan, while slowly developing a middle class, faced innumerable setbacks. An enervating climate, illiteracy, cyclones, floods, poverty, political instability, and an agrarian economy all worked against progress.

Finally, after many military coups and a variety of political and military leaders, a new figure emerged. Sheik Mujibur Rahman, a charismatic, educated, highly articulate Bengali became the champion of the Bengali people, a true father figure to the masses.

In December of 1970, a devastating cyclone—one of the worst in the nation's history—took thousands of lives in East Pakistan. East Pakistan begged West Pakistan for assistance. The West wing possessed sufficient helicopters, personnel, and relief supplies to ease much of the suffering in East Pakistan. But the pleas for help were ignored, and West Pakistan maintained a stony silence. This callous behavior shocked the Bengali people. Weren't the people of West Pakistan fellow Muslims? How could they simply ignore the desperate plight of their fellow countrymen and brothers in the faith?

After this, Sheik Mujib openly defied West Pakistan and called the Bengali people to civil disobedience. He did this in the spirit of India's Mohandas K. (Mahatma) Gandhi, who brought Indian commerce to a standstill whenever he asked India's Hindus to disobey their leaders. Bengalis would have followed the Sheik anywhere. When he called for civil disobedience, the wheels of commerce ground to a halt. Shops and offices closed; trucks, buses, cars, rickshaws, and baby taxis were immobile; people stayed home from work; the country ceased to function.

Shortly after the cyclone of 1970, Sheik Mujib and his political party won a provincial election by a landslide. West Pakistan, totally frustrated by its failure to bring order to the East, declared the election invalid. It was the final blow; East Pakistan refused to bow to West Pakistan's demands any longer.

In a last-minute attempt to bring the recalcitrant province to heel, the government of West Pakistan made dire threats. Tiny, poorly equipped East Pakistan fumed; its people sharpened their machetes. They refused to put up with West Pakistan's surly attitude any longer. Without considering the strength of West Pakistan's military machine, the cost in lives, or the resultant destruction to their country, East Pakistan defiantly declared independence, chose a new name, and hoisted a new flag on every flagpole. It was the beginning of a heartbreaking war that nearly aborted this brave nation before it drew its first breath.

At our station in Malumghat, we heard fearful stories of murder and atrocities. It appeared that the West Pakistani military machine had formed an organized plan to decimate East Pakistan's population. The military targeted professionals, intellectuals, and government workers. West Pakistani soldiers methodically murdered doctors, lawyers, teachers, firemen, policemen, and college students. Then they went on to terrorize village residents.

We heard that as the soldiers moved south, military commanders cordoned off each village. Then they entered the village and asked for "a quota," a specified number of men and boys. The soldiers lined them up—and proceeded to shoot their "quota." Rumors of these massacres prompted men and boys to flee the country in droves, or to hide in the jungle. They stayed in the jungle by day, and sneaked back into the village after dark to check on their families and get food for the next day. Pakistani soldiers stayed off the roads at night, afraid of ambush. Found alone, or in small groups, they might encounter angry villagers and be hacked to death with machetes.

After the war, a teacher in the Bengali school at Malumghat told me that he spent most of the war in the jungle. He and his friends sat and played cards all day. The schools were closed, the boys had nothing else to occupy them, and they were afraid to go home during the day.

Looting became a way of life for evil men during the war. Thieves preyed on village people fleeing the country. Some took everything the evacuees carried, usually food and money desperately needed for the trip. I heard of one thief who relented at the last moment, allowing a tearful mother to keep a precious tin of baby food, without which her baby would have starved.

Various factors led to the evacuation of most of the missionaries from East Pakistan at that time. The American government, unable to predict the behavior of warring armies, wanted them out of harm's way. But it was hard to leave Bengali friends to an uncertain fate. Reid Minich stayed in Chittagong; Drs. Vic Olsen and Donn Ketcham remained at Malumghat. They hoped to protect ABWE's property and help the Bengali community as much as possible.

The rest of us scattered in different directions. Some missionaries, due for furlough, left Chittagong harbor on an evacuation ship, commissioned by the U.S. government. God protected and provided for us wherever we went, and brought us back into the country after a brief exile. All the missionaries, except for those who went to North America, returned to the country within two months, remaining there for the rest of the war. The presence of missionaries in Chittagong and Malumghat helped reduce violence in their immediate vicinity; the Pakistani army was not eager to have its nefarious deeds publicized in the foreign press. We foreigners kept a low profile, but witnessed the genocide of a brave nation. Malumghat was a "pocket of peace" in the midst of a whirling storm. The hospital remained open for business, and God kept us safe.

Thousands of Bengalis were forced to flee East Pakistan in order to save their lives. Most of them crossed the border and camped in large Indian cities like Calcutta. India did what she could to feed, clothe, and protect the refugees, but the war badly overtaxed her own resources. In December 1971, the Indian army made a two-pronged attack on the beleaguered West Pakistani army. The Indians crossed the border into Dacca and moved south. Naval vessels arrived in Cox's Bazar and moved troops north toward Chittagong. Indian commanders broadcast a simple ultimatum to the West Pakistani officers: *Surrender now, or we will destroy you.* The broadcast was chilling. There was no doubt that India would keep her word. Fearing India's military power, the West Pakistani commanders capitulated almost immediately. The brutal war was finally over. Citizens of newly formed Bangladesh pelted the Indian rescuers with flowers, screamed *"Joi Bangla!"* (Victory, Bangladesh!), danced in the streets, and ran up the country's new flag.

nineteen

Mountain Refuge

Leaving Bangladesh at the beginning of the Liberation War was difficult for several reasons. Some ABWE missionaries were working in East Pakistan with expired visas. This was not unusual; visas often expired before the government issued new ones. Missionaries could stay in the country with a "pending" visa, but if we left the country there was no guarantee we could return. It was also hard to leave our Bengali friends behind, not knowing what would happen to them once we left the country.

We had discussed contingency plans in great detail for several weeks. As we viewed the escalating tension in the country, it seemed only a matter of time before East Pakistan exploded into open conflict. When two young men from the American consulate arrived at Malumghat in April 1971, urging us to leave the country, each of us was forced to make a decision. The field council met to listen to the consular officers and discuss our options. The U.S. government was committed to keeping us safe, but with the Pakistan military moving in our direction, the American Consul was unable to ensure our protection.

During one of the meeting breaks, as I stood on the guest house verandah, Becky Davey came out and said, "How's it going? Made a decision yet?"

"Becky, I'm not afraid to stay and I hate to leave, but I don't like putting American soldiers at risk if everything falls apart. If they have to send troops in to rescue us, this place could turn into another Congo. If the U.S. government asks us to leave because they can't protect us, it's a reasonable request. But I certainly don't want to leave East Pakistan without a valid visa."

After more group discussion, I decided to go to West Pakistan with Linda Short and Gwen Geens. Linda hadn't lived in the country for long, and Gwen arrived in Dacca right in the middle of a major cyclone. Both had endured enough psychological trauma to last a lifetime. Friends of mine in Quetta, West Pakistan, would probably take us in. Unless West Pakistan won the war and booted us out of the country, our visas should allow us to return to East Pakistan when the situation cooled down.

Several missionary families and singles were scheduled for furlough, and an American ship in Chittagong harbor stood ready to take them on board. Bob and Barb Adolph, due for vacation, decided to fly to Karachi, West Pakistan, since the U.S. government offered to fly missionaries there to get us out of the country. Bob and Barb didn't want their small children to be in the path of the West Pakistan military moving toward Malumghat.

The caravan of refugees left for Chittagong the next morning, with Reid Minich leading the way on his motorcycle. Several groups of Bengalis along the road stopped our vehicles to ask where we were going. When they learned we were leaving the country, they gave us a message for America. "Please," they pled, "tell your people what's happening to us. Tell the President of the United States that the West Pakistanis are trying to kill us all."

We were saddened by the damage we saw as we traveled north. The carnage increased as we approached Chittagong, and we were shocked by all the bombed-out buildings, scorched fields, and deserted markets. Where were all the people? Chittagong, ordinarily bustling and teeming with people and vehicles, was eerily deserted. War had not yet reached Malumghat, but it had certainly ravaged Chittagong. Jo Spina, an Assembly of God missionary and long-time friend there, served us dinner. The men from the American consulate checked in with their office, then returned to talk to us.

"The consul is not happy that so few of your people left Malumghat," one man said gravely. "He thinks that *all* nonessential personnel should be gone before the Pakistan military gets that far south. The people at Malumghat are too isolated. If anything happened, we'd have trouble getting troops in to evacuate the rest of the missionaries. There was an incident at the Chandraghona mission hospital, and the Consul doesn't want your people to risk meeting up with well-armed soldiers."

"Do you think," the other continued, "that if we broadcast a message on Voice of America (VOA) radio, more of your colleagues would leave the country? We offered to return to Malumghat tomorrow, but the Pakistan Commander refuses to call a truce, even for one day. He thinks your people had their chance; he won't put himself out to help them again."

We discussed it among ourselves and decided it was worth a try. Early the next morning, the men escorted us to the airport. Before we left, we listened to the announcement on Voice of America. It had been aired on the late evening VOA broadcast the night before; now it was broadcast again, giving the Malumghat missionaries two opportunities to hear it. The terse announcement stated, "The road to Chittagong is no longer open. All nonessential Malumghat personnel should leave the country via Burma."

We learned much later that Becky Davey heard the evening VOA broadcast while she was packing her suitcase in case evacuation became necessary. She alerted everyone and, by the second broadcast, all the American personnel at Malumghat—except Donn and Vic—were en route to the Burma border.

Linda, Gwen, and I left for Dacca on a small STOL (short take off and landing) passenger plane. There were not many passengers, and an armed Pakistani guard sat facing us, watching our every move. The stewardess was outwardly calm, but betrayed her inner turmoil by mixing tea and coffee in the same carafe. It didn't matter; all of us were too afraid to move or speak. The guard didn't threaten us, but he kept swinging his gun from side to side. I feared he would fire his gun accidentally, and I breathed a sigh of relief when we landed safely at Dacca airport. The airport, too, was under heavy security as groups of Pakistani soldiers waited for flights to Chittagong. Many of them were tall mountain men who looked as though they had just arrived from the famous Northwest Frontier between Pakistan and Afghanistan.

The consulate arranged seats for Gwen, Linda, and me on a commercial flight to Karachi. Jo Spina's friends in Karachi willingly took us in until I could contact my friends in Quetta. I sent off a note to Dr. Ronnie Holland, and he replied immediately: "Come and stay as long as you like." We flew into Quetta and took a taxi to the mission hospital where Joan and Ronnie Holland lived.

I had met the Hollands during my first term of missionary service when Joyce Wingo and I visited Quetta on holiday. The city is situated high in the rugged mountains of West Pakistan, near the Afghanistan border, a cool, quiet place for vacation. Joyce and I had stayed in a hotel in town, where both of us picked up severe cases of amoeba. Because we needed medication, someone suggested we contact Dr. Ronnie Holland at the eye hospital. Ronnie and Joan took us in, made us welcome, and found us rooms in the nurses' residence. The Hollands were Church Missionary Society (CMS) missionaries from England. Sir Henry Holland, Ronnie's father, a famous pioneer in eye surgery on the Pakistani frontier, opened the eye hospital in Quetta to deal with the thousands of cataracts seen in this remote area. Now Ronnie, an eye surgeon at the hospital, held eye camps, offering free treatment for cataracts, on the plains during the winter when the mountain passes were closed by snow and patients could not reach the hospital. He had grown up in Quetta; it was home to him.

Ronnie's wife, Joan, an incredible woman, was confined to a wheelchair, but there was nothing crippled about her. "Not long after Ronnie and I were married," she explained, "I contracted polio. Ronnie was desperate. He showed his clinic helpers how to do artificial respiration. They kept me alive while Ronnie repaired an ancient respirator. Without the respirator I would have died. Ronnie's mother and father lived at another mission station. When they got Ronnie's wire, they came immediately and took over the clinic work. They helped out as much as possible and were a tremendous encouragement to us."

Ronnie and Joan returned to England until her condition stabilized. Joan smiled at Ronnie and said, "Ronnie was so mean to me. Here I was in a respirator and he dribbled food into my mouth to get me to eat. If I didn't want food all over my face, I had to open my mouth."

Ronnie shook his head and said, "Darling, I had to do something to get you to eat." For a while, Joan didn't really care whether she lived or died, but Ronnie's love and encouragement restored her will to live. Every time Ronnie lifted Joan out of the wheelchair or helped her with some task, the expression on his face showed how much he loved her. She bore three children, learned to give anesthesia so she could help Ronnie in the operating room, kept the hospital books, and was a wonderful wife and mother.

Ronnie and Joan opened their little Volunteer Service Organization (similar to our Peace Corps) cottage for the three of us in 1971, and the other missionaries serving at the eye hospital brought us gifts of food. We had no intention of settling in, but it was nice to have a quiet refuge until things settled down in East Pakistan. The cottage was well-equipped, and we had fun cooking. We also enjoyed eating at the Chinese restaurant and purchasing local delicacies in the market. Our favorite breakfast was scrambled eggs wrapped in warm *"nan ruti,"* flat bread made in a brick oven. One of us scrambled eggs, while the other two raced to the *bazar* for *nan ruti* hot out of the oven.

Ronnie enjoyed showing us the area surrounding the hospital.

His father had built a cottage in the mountains above Quetta many years earlier. The climate in the mountains is so dry that wood doesn't deteriorate. Ronnie and Joan drove us up to the cottage for a brief visit. The view was incredible—rugged mountains in every direction. Fragrant juniper branches hung from the verandah ceiling. It was just a simple wooden cabin, but it provided a serene spot for a busy doctor and his family to vacation.

Ronnie never left Joan behind when he went into the villages to visit tribal chiefs or patients. One day he said, "Joan and I are going out to visit a tribal chief. We'll take a picnic lunch with us, and we'd like you to come along." The people we visited were shepherds, nomads who herded goats. They live in tents in the mountains as long as the weather is mild. When the weather begins to grow cold, they gather their goats and go down to the plains before snow traps them in the mountains for the long winter.

I wondered how Ronnie managed to move Joan in places where using a wheelchair is not an option, and I found that he made simple work of it. When we got to the tribal village, Ronnie sat Joan on a blanket and four strong men picked up the corners and carried her into the village. I asked Joan if being carried that way was scary. She laughed and said, "We've been doing it that way for so long, I don't even think about it. If Ronnie hadn't thought of something, I would have missed so much of the children's growing up. They used to worry about me, even when they went swimming. They hated the fact that I couldn't go in the water with them, but they were happy when I could go on picnics and outings. Even with the children away, I go with Ronnie whenever I'm able to do so."

Linda, Gwen, and I were amazed at the tribal women in their bright, heavily embroidered dresses and baggy pants. They certainly didn't look like any Pakistani women we'd ever seen, with their fair skin, rosy cheeks, auburn hair, and blue or hazel eyes. The women were as fascinated by us as we were by them. We couldn't stop staring at each other. Ronnie looked at the expressions on our faces and said, "Ever hear of Alexander the Great? You're looking at some of the women he left behind when he swept through this area." It was a living history lesson we'd remember for a long time.

The day we were to leave Quetta for Karachi, we awoke to a dust storm. Ronnie took us to the airport, but he figured the plane probably wouldn't fly with such poor visibility. He was right; our flight was cancelled. On the way back to the cottage, Ronnie quipped, "I have known daring pilots and I have known old pilots, but I have never known a daring, *old* pilot." We decided we'd rather not fly through a dust storm with a daring pilot—or an old pilot either, for that matter.

Ronnie helped us make arrangements to reach Karachi by overnight train. We laughed about it later, but that night it was no laughing matter. We almost froze to death on the air-conditioned train. Nobody told us we needed to rent blankets and pillows *before* the train left Quetta. We pulled out all the warm clothing in our suitcases, but still spent the night shivering. That changed the moment we reached Karachi and discovered that the temperature was almost 100°.

While we waited for flights to East Pakistan to resume, Jo Spina's friends asked us to teach at a Daily Vacation Bible School sponsored by several area churches. That was fun, since most of the teenage girls spoke more Urdu than English. The girls loved the classes, and it was good to be involved in ministry again.

The day finally came when we bought tickets on a commercial flight to Dacca. Conditions had stabilized enough that it was safe to return home. We knew the war was not over when we saw the large number of military officers on the airplane. They wore business suits but lined up to deposit their pistols with security before boarding the plane. We had been gone for two months. Traveling from Chittagong to Malumghat by bus was depressing. So many villages had disappeared; so many homes had been destroyed; so many rice fields were overgrown. We were grieved by what had happened to the country in our brief absence.

God took our missionaries to safety in various places, and now He had brought us back together. He took care of our Bengali friends, even though many of them had fled to the hills. Several Christian missions close to the Indian border were looted and badly damaged when war raged around them. God preserved all our assets in Chittagong and at Malumghat; nothing was lost or destroyed. He provided everything we needed, and enabled us to keep the hospital open throughout the rest of the war.

twenty

A Bittersweet Experience

The ABWE missionaries who lived in Chittagong and Malumghat were involved in relief operations both during and after the 1971 war. Chittagong suffered extensive damage. Missionaries there had their share of refugees, vanishing commodities, whizzing bullets, and daily trials. Malumghat, more than sixty miles south and off the beaten track, faced struggles different from those in Chittagong, but no less traumatic or difficult since we possessed few resources or solutions to the many problems we encountered.

Relief agencies brought in tons of food, bedding, donated clothing and other supplies, and looked to the missionaries to help distribute these goods to the needy. At Malumghat, we set up a carefully monitored relief program, designed to distribute adequate food to those in our area. Many Bengali people would have been destitute without the food and goods we were able to pass along.

The MCH compound overflowed with homeless people for months. Hospital staff did their best to provide rice, clothing, housing, and medical care to everyone in need. Mothers often arrived with teenage daughters clinging to them. They were afraid of the West Pakistani soldiers whose convoys were moving south from Chittagong into the rural areas. The bad reputation of the military machine preceded their southward trek. As the soldiers advanced, many Bengali men fled, leaving the village women and girls without protection.

Dacoits (bandits) victimized wealthy villagers. The hospital saw its share of grief in those dark days. I remember the day a little girl was brought in for surgery. Bandits entered her village home during the night. They beat on the door with rifle butts, but the terrified family refused to open the door. The bandits pulled back part of the sheet metal roof and shot down into the house below. The little girl was in the line of fire. Her life was spared, but she lost an eye to a band of greedy, depraved men.

That rainy season was one of the wettest I can remember. As we single missionary women gathered for breakfast each morning, we wondered how many Bengalis had spent the night under trees in the jungle. Many were afraid to stay at home and had nowhere to go but the jungle.

At the hospital, we treated several cases of nephritis, a kidney inflammation brought on by exposure to rain and cold. One Hindu family brought in their little boy, his body puffy and his eyes swollen shut. He needed a specific antibiotic in a child's dosage. Our supply line for medicines from Chittagong no longer existed, nor could we import medicines from other countries. Donn Ketcham asked me to check the MCH pharmacy for the antibiotic the child needed. I shook my head. Impossible. Then I checked, and although I'm not sure where it came from, there it sat on the shelf, one bottle of the exact antibiotic syrup the child needed. I have often wondered if the little boy's guardian angel put it on the shelf while my back was turned. Just one bottle was enough to turn the tide for him. He was soon up and around, trotting along behind the staff as we made rounds.

We devised strict rules about who was eligible for relief food. Each person received a new ticket every week. No ticket, or the *wrong* ticket, meant no food allotment. The lines were long, since each family's food was carefully measured into a sack or basket. We were never sure we'd have enough food for everyone in line. One day, the lines were unusually long and everyone tired of waiting. But our helpers had to measure out the food according to the number of family members on each ticket.

A little girl came through the line, presented her ticket, and held out her basket to be filled. We issued a new ticket every week, and her ticket was the wrong color! Upon hearing this, she burst into tears. I have no idea why she had the wrong ticket, but I said, "Go ahead, give her the food anyhow." I couldn't bear to see the child walk away with an empty basket and no food.

The village women who appeared at MCH for food week after week wore simple cotton saris, often in shades of deep blue or green. Hindu widows traditionally wear white. White saris stay white only as long as they are washed with soap. Bengali villagers use a strong lye soap that keeps the saris white. During the war when soap was scarce, money to buy soap was even scarcer. It seemed like everything turned gray. The villagers were gray with grief, worry, and fear; unwashed saris turned gray; and the skies were leaden with rain clouds.

We did see some sunlight, however. God wonderfully supplied the needs of missionaries and the Bengali believers. Christians returning from Burma after the war told of God's miraculous protection. He supplied their material needs even though they didn't know anyone in Burma.

As Mennonite families in America prepared to celebrate Christmas that year, they remembered the suffering people in war-torn Bangladesh and prepared wonderful bundles for children. They pinned each bundle inside a new bath towel with big, shiny safety pins. Each bundle contained a child's dress or suit, toiletries, and a small toy. Some folks had sewn name and address tags on the outside, so we knew where the bundles originated. Each person who contributed a bundle also contributed a dollar. The money helped speed the bundles to needy children on the other side of the world. The Mennonite Central Committee sent many of those bundles to Malumghat hospital. They also blessed us abundantly with large barrels of Mennonite specialties: canned meat, handmade laundry soap, beautiful quilts, warm sweaters, and baby layettes. What a wonderful way those families chose to thank God for the indescribable gift of His dear Son!

The day our Christian refugees arrived home, I went through several barrels to see what I could find for them. My eyes filled with tears as I pulled out quilts, blankets, sweaters, baby clothes, and children's bundles. The Mennonites had packed everything we needed in those barrels. God met *our* needs through those generous people. I will always be grateful for the time, energy, and money these friends invested in people they will never see until heaven.

The war also provided many opportunities to present the gospel. People were terribly frightened, not knowing whether they would ever see their families again. Many of them lost homes and possessions to fire or looters. Some weren't even sure they would survive the war.

Because many women appeared at MCH once a week for food supplies, Shabi and I decided it was a good time to hold Bible classes. I prepared a series of five lessons that highlighted the life of Christ and clearly presented the plan of salvation. Shabi taught the class every week. We encouraged the women to listen to the series as often as they wished. Some sat through the series multiple times. They would say, "I don't understand yet" or "I need to hear the stories again." A number of ladies were saved through that contact. We were thankful that God made it possible for us to present the gospel while their hearts were tender to its message.

When independence finally reached East Pakistan in December 1971, families had been decimated; homes were reduced to piles of rubble; the economy was in shambles. Some wives never learned what became of their husbands; many of those who fled to India never returned. Others lost their lives in West Pakistan's first military push or during the military occupation. Some villages near MCH had no male residents after the war. They either had been killed by firing squads or lost in the exodus to India.

The world wondered if the tiny, battered, bloodstained country that became Bangladesh could survive. But this land has practiced survival techniques for years, overcoming tidal waves, cyclones, earthquakes, droughts, and other disasters. Freedom came with a high price tag, but victory must have tasted sweet after the long, bitter struggle for independence.

twenty-one

A Day at the Beach

In the summer of 1971, after all the missionaries who had evacuated to various countries returned to Bangladesh, we began to feel as though we were in prison. We were not really prisoners, but as the war moved south, drawing closer and closer to the area near MCH, the missionary men thought it unsafe for women to leave the compound. A steady stream of military vehicles passed Memorial Christian Hospital on their way south. Fearing ambush, the West Pakistani vehicles treated another moving vehicle as though it were invisible. If it did not move out of the way immediately, they simply rammed the vehicle and pushed it off the road. In enemy territory, the West Pakistani military were vulnerable to attack and took no chances. Because they were vulnerable, we were vulnerable, too; so women had to remain on the mission compound. Freedom becomes especially sweet when you lose it.

Christmas was quickly approaching and the morning of December 4 dawned bright and sunny. Linda Short, short-term teacher Jewl Spoelhof, and I asked for a day pass. "Please," we pleaded, "the road has been clear for days. We just want to drive to Cox's Bazar, do some Christmas shopping, and spend a little time at the beach. We won't be gone long, and we'll be back before dark." Perhaps we looked as if we were about to succumb to cabin fever. The men talked it over at length, gave us permission to leave the compound, and insisted we *must* be home well before dark.

We grabbed bathing suits, towels, and money, and raced for

the car before they could change their minds! Besides, if we were to be back before dark, we had no time to waste. We saw almost no traffic on the road for the thirty-mile trip to Cox's Bazar, so we made good time in our little VW bug. Soldiers manned guard posts along the road, but none flagged us down to ask us who we were or where we were going. We pulled into Cox's, a sleepy seaside town, and prepared to head for the beach. First things first, of course.

As soon as I set foot on the sidewalk, a Bengali man approached me, smiling broadly. "Sister," he said, "it is so good to see you. You haven't been in Cox's for months, have you? Please, Sister," he continued, "you and your friends must come to my house for tea. My wife will be so happy to see you. She is so much better and so thankful for the care she received in your hospital. She will be very disappointed if you don't visit her while you are here."

Those of us who worked in the hospital often ran into former patients and their families in Cox's Bazar. I spoke softly to Jewl, "I know we don't have much time, but we *have* to go to his house. He will never understand if I refuse. That would be really rude."

We accepted his invitation with as much grace as we could manage. I drove the car to his house and parked in the front yard. Linda, Jewl, and I visited over warm Cokes, *chana chur* (a spicy snack mix), and cookies. His wife chatted cheerfully, happy that she felt so much better. We finally said our farewells and left, this time heading for the nearby market. Our Bengali friend insisted we leave the VW in his yard. "Don't try to park in the *bazar*," he said. "Your car will be safer here."

By now, it was so late that we probably wouldn't have time to swim; we'd have to decide after we bought the things we needed for Christmas. We walked into a *dokhan* (bamboo market stall) and began to look at wrapped sweets and small items we could use as Christmas gifts for our Bengali friends.

Suddenly, the engine of an airplane throbbed overhead. How strange! Commercial planes had not flown in or out of Cox's Bazar for months. What was going on? Linda poked her head out of the doorway to investigate. When I looked over her shoulder, I spotted an Indian fighter plane, diving toward the *bazar*. And it was not just *one* plane; there were at least seven. I pulled Linda back inside the shop.

The small, metal-roofed, thatched building that housed the shop would not provide much protection from strafing or rockets. For one horrible moment, I thought the shopkeeper was going to push us out into the street. That is exactly what he did to his Bengali customers, who were forced to take refuge in drains along the road. Calmly, the owner put up the boards that formed the front of his shop. Then he motioned to the three of us to sit on the stools in front of his counter. We sat in semi-darkness, trying to figure out what was happening. Although we could hear the *crump* of rockets falling and the staccato beat of machine gun strafing, we had no idea what the planes were targeting.

Jewl, Linda, and I thought we were facing certain death in that flimsy little *dokhan*. Though we did not pray out loud, our hearts lifted in silent entreaty to God. After about ten minutes, the rocketing and strafing stopped. The noise outside now was the sound of frightened people scurrying down the street. Linda turned to Jewl and me and said with the utmost sincerity, "I think we ought to pray."

Jewl and I burst out laughing. "Linda, you goose," we said, "what do you think we've *been* doing for the past ten minutes?" We were grateful for God's protection, but Linda's solemn pronouncement cracked us up. At any rate, her comment broke the tension.

We expressed our appreciation to the shopkeeper for his kindness, quickly paid for our purchases, and ran for the car. Bengalis, fleeing in the other direction, tried to stop us, insisting that we were courting self-destruction. We ignored them, knowing our car was parked just down the street. Our host greeted us when we rushed into his yard. He had been concerned for our safety, knowing that we were shopping in the *bazar*. After thanking him again for his hospitality, we jumped in the car and headed for home. My Bengali friends in Cox's Bazar teased me for months about that fast get-away. They all thought it was amazing that mine was the first car out of town after the raid!

We had several major concerns. We were not sure what damage the planes had inflicted—or where—and we were sure our missionary colleagues heard the raid from Malumghat. Was the road still open, or had rockets damaged it? Had the planes hit targets other than the *bazar*? We knew our co-workers would be anxious, not knowing if we were safe, injured, or unable to leave Cox's Bazar.

Not one of the guard posts on our homeward route was manned. The guards ran for their lives when they saw Indian fighter planes approaching Cox's Bazar. We roared up the highway, eager to reach the safety of the MCH compound, arriving just in time to head off the convoy of missionary vehicles venturing out to search for us. Hearing the bombs and rockets had scared the wits out of them! They not only knew the three of us were in Cox's Bazar, but also were afraid we might have been lounging on the beach when the attack took place.

Ah yes, we planned to go to the beach, didn't we? The Lord directed our steps that day and kept us away from the beach. We learned later that the planes had strafed and rocketed the airport, just a few short blocks from the *bazar*. They also strafed the harbor and the electric light plant on the edge of town. It was the beginning of a full-scale Indian army attack on the southern end of the country. The planes were softening up the area before the Indian army launched an invasion by sea. And we were on hand to witness their first attack!

After that adventure, we no longer considered ourselves prisoners. Home had never looked so good, and we were happy to settle down in the comparative safety of our compound.

Several months later, a group of Indian officers camped near Malumghat. One day an officer came to my dental room for treatment. As we talked, I mentioned that I had been shopping in Cox's Bazar with friends the day Indian planes strafed and rocketed the town. He looked at me in disbelief and asked shakily, "You were there?"

"Oh, yes," I replied. "We were in the *bazar* when the planes strafed and rocketed the airport. We watched the planes dive over the town. They were quite close to where we were. Actually, we were in a *dokhan* and it was rather scary."

He turned a sickly color and said, "Madam, I assure you we did not rocket and strafe Cox's Bazar. You must be mistaken." Intent on saving face, he turned and beat a hasty retreat from my office.

twenty-two

New Directions

At the time of the 1971 war, no one knew Bangladesh would win. A poor, provincial country with no military power and a shaky economy could not possibly afford an extended conflict. What would happen to the missionaries if West Pakistan won the war? God had given our mission good rapport with government officials in East Pakistan. We had encountered visa problems along the way, but the government usually treated us graciously. We were not sure this attitude would prevail if West Pakistan won the war. I think we all asked the same questions. What would we leave behind if we were forced to evacuate the country permanently? Was the Bengali church viable? Could the Bengali Christians stand firm in a hostile environment?

My single women missionary colleagues and I contributed to a variety of ministries. We were nurses, schoolteachers, and Bible women who ministered to Bengali women and children. All of us had Bible school training as well as other skills and experience. Each of us was involved in some aspect of evangelism and church planting. As we sat and voiced concerns about the needs of Bengali women, we realized that we had not capitalized on their strengths. Linda said, "What we need to do is teach them to reach their own people with the gospel. We won't be here forever. Unless we develop trained leaders, we *won't* leave anything behind." That was a scary thought. But how could we teach the women? We were already up to our eyebrows in work!

As we discussed the need to train Bengali women, I realized that I had been spoon-feeding Shabi. Perhaps I could at least correct *that* mistake. I had carefully taught her each lesson, then listened to her repeat the story to me. When I thought she was ready, Shabi taught the story on the female ward at the hospital or at a village Bible class. I needed to cut her loose from my apron strings. This promised to be an interesting experiment, but Shabi was a smart girl and I was eager to see what she could do by herself.

I prepared her next Bible lesson in simple Bengali. She came into my office, expecting me to teach her the lesson the way I always had. Instead, I said, "Shabi, I'm very busy today. Why don't you take the lesson and study it yourself? Let me know if you have any questions. When you're ready to teach the story, come back and tell it to me. Okay?"

She took the material and went away to study. A few days later she returned and told me the story like an old pro. I was proud of her (and ashamed of me). "Shabi," I said, "you can teach that lesson right now in the female ward. When I'm finished here, I'll come help with the singing."

She sat in the chair opposite my desk and looked at me without smiling. "I know what you are doing," Shabi said, "but it's all right. Come when you are ready. I can teach the story myself." She got up from her chair, flashed her mischievous smile, and went to the ward. Did I really think I could put one over on her? Shabi didn't have much education, but she was sharp as a tack. I guess it was her old spiritual "mom" who was a bit slow on the uptake!

Becky, Linda Short, and I decided to try a pilot project, teaching the Bengali women who seemed most interested in learning biblical truths. Some were nurses with high school education; others had less education, but a keen desire to learn. Anyone who enrolled in the class had to be literate, an essential requirement for their success. Linda spearheaded the program. The rest of us helped prepare and teach the materials. It was hard work, but well worth the effort. The students soaked up Bible truth like sponges.

It was exciting to see the ladies take God's Word literally. Mary, one of the students, rushed to the hospital one day, toting a huge bag full of mangoes from her own garden. She dropped her load beside me, wiped her brow, and said breathlessly, "Sister, I have to sell these mangoes in the market right now!"

"Mary," I teased, "what's the rush? They won't spoil *that* fast!"

She insisted, "I just read the story of Ananias and Sapphira in my Bible. I promised these mangoes to God if He gave us a good crop. I'm afraid something might happen before I can sell them. I don't want to end up like Sapphira!"

I was tempted to laugh, but Mary was serious. She had a keen desire to fulfill her promise to God. She took her mangoes to the *bazar* right then so she could pay her obligation to the Lord, which is not a bad attitude for any Christian to imitate.

One of the courses I taught was the book of Romans. Much of it was new to the women, and they applied it seriously to their own lives. One morning Mary entered the classroom and accusingly asked, "Are you a Jew?"

"No," I said, "I'm no more Jewish than you are. We have one missionary who is part Jewish. Mr. Golin has a Jewish father, so he's half-Jewish. Why do you ask?"

Mary explained that she had been reading straight through the book of Romans, one of the class requirements. When she reached Chapter 11, she discovered God's great love for the Jewish people. She was heartbroken. "I thought that God loved me more than anything. Then I found out that He really loves the Jews more than He loves anyone else."

"Mary," I said, "I guess God really does love us a lot. He does love the Jewish people, but He also loved us enough to send Jesus Christ to die for our sins." She understood that God loved her, but I'm not sure she ever forgave Larry Golin for being part Jewish. Mary thought that being Jewish must be the most wonderful thing in the world. Imagine being Jewish and knowing Jesus Christ at the same time!

The tests Becky, Linda, and I gave were difficult, so we were surprised at how well the women performed. To them, missing a final exam was just about the worst thing that could happen! One morning, as I prepared to pass out final-exam papers, a young schoolboy appeared at the classroom door. He was looking for his mother, who was one of my students. He had severe diarrhea and thought he needed her.

Much to my surprise, she turned to me and said, "Please, go get his grandfather. He's downstairs." She did not say anything else, but the look on her face told me she had no intention of missing her exam.

Obediently, I ran downstairs, called the grandfather and explained what had transpired. Then I ran back upstairs and handed out the exam papers. Everyone passed, including one mom with a very soggy little boy.

Practical work was an important aspect of the training program. Some women taught village Bible classes, while others witnessed on MCH's female ward. Some of the students proved to be excellent teachers. One day I listened to a student tell a Bible story on the female ward, delighted at the poise with which she taught and the winning way she had with the local women. We began to believe that we *could* have a viable church and a trained leadership if the missionaries ever had to leave the country. It was a good feeling.

We worked hard with the students and rejoiced in their progress. Eventually, the Bengali Christian men began to ask, "Why isn't someone teaching us? The women are learning so much. They come home and tell us what they have learned. We want to study the Bible, too."

That was another beginning, as Linda Short and a team of missionaries prepared curriculum to teach God's Word to both men and women. And so, trained leaders were developed within the church at Malumghat. This was a wonderful spin-off from the devastation of 1971. God opened our eyes to the need for training and helped us put a program together. The Bible school multiplied our gospel witness and expanded our outreach into many previously unevangelized areas. It was our own private revolution. The result was a core group of trained pastors and Bible women, able and willing to take the gospel to their own people.

Women at Heart House create macramé handbags.

Heart House workers prepare dolls in a cottage industry setting.

Prova fashions a costume doll.

A Heart House worker uses a hand-operated sewing machine.

Kanan (left) and another woman sew at Heart House.

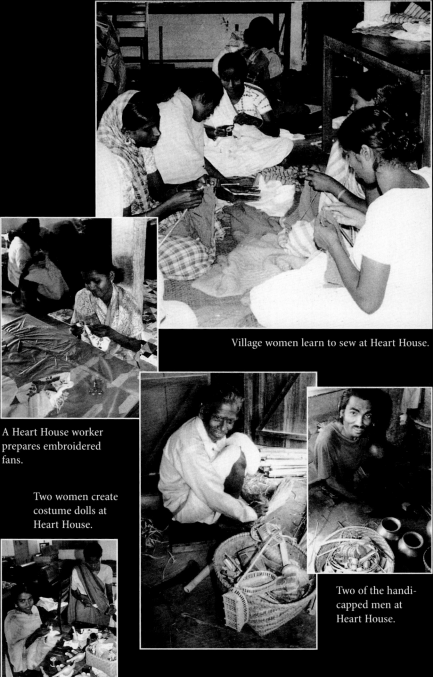

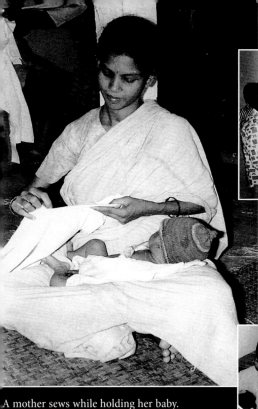

School boys at the Bengali Christian School at Malumghat play karoms during recess.

Students sharpen their skills at Primary School.

A mother sews while holding her baby.

Youngsters prepare for a school picnic.

Manik and three high school teachers at a sports award ceremony.

A young student at Malumghat solves a difficult problem.

Children at the Malumghat school sing an action chorus.

Mary Lou with Malumghat students.

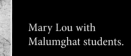

t w e n t y - t h r e e

Heart House

Malumghat missionaries, with the help of Bengali staff members, gave out huge quantities of relief supplies during the 1971 war. But once the war was over, we wanted life to return to normal. Having to accept relief is demeaning; having to give relief is draining. We knew from long experience that our Bengali neighbors needed to work for their rice and curry. Measuring out rice for them week after week would not help them rebuild their self-esteem. We needed to shift our focus from delivering relief to developing self-sufficiency. During the war, we fed and clothed many women and girls left destitute when their husbands and fathers fled the country. Some of them were local residents, while others came from distant villages. We were the last hope for many of them. If we did not help, they had nowhere else to turn. After the war, some of them had no home to go back to and nowhere else to go.

Bengali culture's unwritten rule is that family members, no matter how distant the relationship, are always welcome in the home of a relative with sufficient means to feed and house them. We missionaries often shook our heads, knowing that some of our hospital employees suffered real hardship when a relative came to "visit" and stayed for an indefinite time. It caused such serious problems that we limited guest visits in hospital staff housing to two weeks. At the end of two weeks, the relative had to leave. We didn't want our hospital employees exploited just because they were industrious enough to find jobs.

All that changed abruptly after the war. As I talked to people who needed relief, I often heard the words, "I stayed at my sister's house until her husband gathered up my belongings and told me to take my baby and leave. He put my bundle on the road and said he couldn't feed me any longer. Please help me. I have nowhere else to go."

The brother-in-law was not being deliberately cruel. He was forced to choose. He and his wife and children could share what little they had, spreading their resources so thin that no one survived, or he could refuse to share, and thereby ensure his family's survival. Some men even abandoned their families when they could no longer feed them.

After the war, the missionaries at Malumghat were left with a group of local women unable to support themselves. The hospital relief program fed them for months, but who would support them now that the war was over? Choices for an indigent woman were extremely limited. During rice harvest, she might hire herself out to help gather, dry, and winnow the rice crop in exchange for food and a place to sleep. But if this woman had a baby in her arms and toddlers clinging to her, no one would hire her. She wouldn't be able to do enough work to make hiring her worthwhile. She was dependent on the dubious charity of those in her village. Prostitution might be her only option if she wanted to survive and feed her children. Demeaning, indeed.

I made a rash statement every other day or so. It went something like this: "I am not going to give relief to these people indefinitely. If we don't want to see them turn into beggars, we have to stop giving them relief. I know it's a complicated problem, but we must find a solution."

Every time I made the statement, Donn Ketcham would say, "Lou, I wish you'd stop talking and do something!" I wanted to, but I didn't know what to do. MCH planned to shut down its relief program since most of the local people had returned to their villages and fields. But there was still a group of women who, because they had lost their homes and husbands in the war, continued to depend on us. How would they care for their children unless they worked? How would they live? How could we help them? The problem seemed endlessly complicated to me.

Malumghat station council discussed the possibility of starting a small pilot work project. Could we teach these women a trade? A group of American college students traveled to Bangladesh to help rebuild houses destroyed in the war. As they prepared to go home, I screwed up my courage and approached Ed Myer, the group's money manager, to ask if they had a few leftover dollars. I explained what we had in mind, and asked, "Ed, do you have any money left that I could put into women's rehabilitation?"

Ed thought for a minute, and said, "I can let you have $1,000. Would that help?"

That would more than help! It was a wonderful nest egg that built a little brick house in the middle of the hospital compound. We painted the doors, window frames, and shutters bright red and hung a sign that read Heart House. Many people have asked me why I called it Heart House. It's hard to explain, but I felt that this little house needed a very big heart for those in need. It also sounds good in Bengali. Strangely enough, Bengalis never questioned the meaning. I think they knew that the little house with red shutters had a great big heart.

Relief agencies were generous in donating treadle sewing machines, fabric, and other supplies. I taught basic sewing techniques, aided by Bengali women skilled in cutting fabric without patterns. Perhaps Heart House could sell children's clothing and women's blouses in the local market.

I learned that I had to keep several things in mind when deciding on Heart House projects. Sewing projects for indigent women were springing up all over Bangladesh. As large quantities of clothing hit the market, prices plummeted. How could all these women possibly make a living? Bengalis ordinarily buy just enough clothing to get by: a set of clothes to wear, a set to wash, and a set of good clothes stored in a metal box. Kids generally wore the same clothes (if they wore clothes at all) until they fell apart or seams couldn't be let out anymore. I had to diversify Heart House's operation if the project was to survive. But how?

On one of my trips to the capital city of Dhaka, I visited the Design Center, developed by the government to teach Bengalis crafts and skills such as painting, leather-working, ceramics, and doll-making. The doll-making intrigued me. Instructors showed a group of women how to make beautifully costumed dolls displaying Bengali culture and customs. When I asked the director about her program, she told me that it was free. The director would personally train someone from my workshop if she lived in Dhaka for two months. It would be my job to find her a place to live and pay her expenses while she learned the craft.

I reasoned that marketing dolls might be difficult, but it couldn't be any worse than marketing clothing in a glutted market. Foreigners—the only people in Bangladesh with money to spend—would be the target purchasers of these goods. Doll-making seemed like an ideal project for Heart House. But who could I send to Dhaka for training? If I chose the wrong person, I couldn't afford a second choice. As I thought and prayed about possibilities, two women came to mind. One was a young single woman without any family ties. The other was a young war widow with several small children.

A British friend of mine worked in a training program called The Jute Works, designed for indigent women. The workshop taught these women to make items such as macramé plant hangers from jute thread. This British lady, a gifted artist, had a great deal more experience with indigent women than I did. The first thing she said was, "Don't make the mistake of sending a young single woman to Dhaka. These girls live at the YWCA and go wild. They are used to life in a village and don't know how to handle freedom. They get into all kinds of trouble."

Hers was just the advice I needed. I went back to Malumghat

and talked to Prova, the young war widow who had come to the mission for help. I explained the doll-making program and said that Heart House would pay all her expenses to go to Dhaka for training. Prova eagerly accepted this opportunity; she eventually became a very talented doll-maker and team leader. Under her direction, the team she selected quickly learned the intricate steps of crafting dolls. Several disabled men, who worked at Heart House crafting small bamboo parts for another project, fashioned tiny objects, such as miniature rolling pins and baskets, that would give life to these culturally accurate dolls. We made all kinds of dolls, from farmers and their wives to lavishly decorated Hindu brides and grooms. Prova painted each delicate doll face with her sensitive hands. It amazed me to see how the team perfectly proportioned the tiny pieces for each display. As missionaries requested special dolls that reflected their particular ministry or something of interest they had seen, the team designed just the right doll, clothing, and cultural setting. A local carpenter fashioned wooden bases of various shapes and sizes, and each completed model was firmly attached to a highly polished base.

Watching the different Heart House teams at work humbled me. One group embroidered hand fans, patterned on a style used in the country for many years. The men bent special cane frames for the fans; then the women assembled the fans, adding delicate finishing touches. Viewed from either side, the ladies' embroidery was beautiful.

Gramma Rizz, Dr. Joe DeCook's mom, taught the Heart House ladies macramé when she visited MCH. Out of that class came handbags, intricately woven from jute thread and lined with colorful jute fabric. The ladies sat on the floor, tying knot after knot, their eyes anywhere but on their work.

The doll-makers showed equal skill. They did everything by eye alone, rarely having to measure. The wire and cotton batting fit snugly into pre-sewn fabric arms and legs. Tiny clothes emerged from the sewing machine, ready to dress each doll in the right costume. The only real problem I dealt with was color. Western ideas of colors and patterns differ greatly from that of the Bengalis. I had to be firm if I wanted color combinations that would appeal to a foreign clientele.

Heart House's doll project took wings and flew! Dolls were made to order for missionaries all over Bangladesh. Later, Heart House shipped dolls to Chittagong and Dhaka where they were, in turn, sold to overseas suppliers. The fans, jute handbags, and dolls were popular items that paid the bills and gave the Heart House employees—mostly women—a living wage.

Heart House also proved itself an excellent evangelistic tool. The women, from Hindu and Buddhist homes, had never heard the gospel before, but some of them found Christ through this ministry of compassion. When I served short-term in Bangladesh after retiring from full-time missions, Margaret Archibald held a camp for local women. Much to my surprise, a group of Heart House ladies went to that event, and several of them were saved. These were ladies who had shown no interest in the gospel during the years I directed Heart House; now their faces beamed as they told me they had found Christ at camp. I was delighted that I was present to rejoice with them. Some of them had hesitated to become Christians because they feared persecution in their villages. It is not easy to live as a believer in a heathen village. It takes great courage and trust in God when you face mockery and intimidation from family and neighbors day after day. And unless these new believers become part of a strong Christian fellowship, they have the haunting fear that no one will be around to offer them comfort in illness, or to bury them when they die.

Heart House has changed over the years. Diversification is still important to its vitality. Jimmie Nusca, a professional seamstress, taught the ladies to make beautiful embroidered clothing. Bengali hand puppets and crocheted lace were added to the list of items for sale. Jimmie's husband, Bob, helped her market Heart House products in new markets throughout the country.

When I visited Bangladesh in 1994, Heart House was still in business more than twenty years after it started, thanks to the leadership of missionaries like Sue James and Alves Weirman. Indigent women still walk through its red doors, looking for training that will help them care for their families. A small on-site shop at Malumghat, as well as many stores in Chittagong, Dhaka, and Cox's Bazar, sell Heart House products. I have often said that God must love those poor Bengali women a whole lot more than I do. In fact, I'm sure of it, because He has supplied our needs and nurtured our ladies for a long time.

twenty-four

The Doll Lady—Prova's Story

Streams of desperate Bengalis passed through MCH's gates during the 1971 war. Driven from their homes, they wandered from place to place, searching for somewhere to stay and something to eat. Perhaps you think you would never "grow weary in well doing," but listening to destitute people every day for months on end might just change your mind.

Actually, listening was only part of the problem. The fact that we had such limited resources caused much of our grief. At the hospital, we gave people food, clothing, and housing, but this was only a temporary solution. Many of these people would eventually go home and resume their normal lives. But what about the women whose husbands had been killed in the war?

When I first met Prova, I saw just one more careworn Bengali woman standing at my office door, with one little boy clinging to her sari and another boy draped over her arm. He looked too big to carry, and I wondered why she held him. She stood for a moment, just looking at me, perhaps too weary to speak. Finally, she said, "My son is sick and I have nowhere to go." Her voice trembled and she seemed on the verge of tears.

I motioned for her and the children to come in and sit down. Then I asked the usual questions, trying to find out what she really wanted. Prova lived at least twenty-five miles north of Memorial Christian Hospital. She lives almost as close to Chittagong as to here, I thought. I wonder what she's doing this far south.

"Prova," I said, "you're a long way from home. Why did you

come all the way down here? Did you come to the hospital for treatment?" She nodded, pointing to the pale little boy now seated in her lap.

"I came to see the doctor," she said, her voice quavering. "He says this one has tuberculosis. I have to come back every month for his medicine but I can't do that. I don't have enough money for bus fare. If I have to come here for medicine, I must find a place to stay. We can't stay in the hotel. It costs too much money. Please, can't you find us a place to stay until my son is better?"

Prova was obviously thinking out loud, working her way through the implications of her son's illness. I was tired. Tired of the endless stream of supplicants, tired of our lack of resources, and tired of not having the answers I needed. I felt lost in a maze. How would I ever find my way to the other end?

All available housing at the hospital was full and I was at a loss to know how to help Prova. "I just can't help you right now. We have no housing for anyone at the moment. I'm afraid you'll have to go home. When you come back for medicine next month, come and see me. Meanwhile, I'll try to work something out for you and the children."

Nodding wearily, she picked up her small son and left my office. The rebuke to my spirit followed almost instantly. God reminded me that nothing was too hard for Him. If I had asked Him, He would have given me His help and wisdom. Why did I think I had to do everything by myself? It was as if He said, Prova is on the verge of a nervous breakdown. In her fragile condition she may not last for another month. How will you feel then?

My heart had been grieved for Prova, but not grieved enough to try to move mountains to help her. Weariness was a poor excuse for my inactivity. I asked the Lord to forgive me and to help me find housing for Prova. I prayed fervently that He would watch over her. And please, dear Lord, I prayed, keep Prova from doing anything foolish. Those kids really need her.

You can imagine my relief when Prova once again stood

outside my office a month later. This time she was smiling, confident that I had found an answer to her dilemma. "Yes," she said in answer to my inquiry, "my little boy is much better. The pills have really helped him." The doctor had given her free medicine and she was grateful.

"Prova," I began, "there is just one empty room in a Bengali staff house. You may stay as long as necessary. The women in the house share a cookhouse, where you can cook for yourself and the children. You won't have to eat at the hotel." I showed her the tiny room in a bamboo house where several destitute women lived with their children. Prova and her children smiled in gratitude.

Several months later, after she knew me better, Prova told me her story. She and her Hindu husband lived in a village close to the highway. During the war, her husband continued working as a bus conductor. The bus driver usually dropped him off near home at the end of the day's run. One day when Prova's husband didn't arrive home at the usual time, Prova became worried because she knew that Hindus were not safe traveling around the country. Hindus were sometimes pulled off the buses by Muslim Pakistani soldiers and marched off to military camps. Some of them disappeared—no one knew what had happened to them. Rumors of atrocities committed on Hindus were widespread, but if her husband did not work, the family would not eat. Perhaps he thought he'd be safe on a public bus. I think he must have been a brave man just to go to work every day. Most of the Hindu men in that area had already fled to India, but Prova's husband was afraid to leave his wife and boys alone. He wanted to take care of them as long as possible.

The following day, a Muslim neighbor came to Prova's house to tell her what had happened. He had a hard time describing the incident. "I saw your husband yesterday," he began. "He was on the bus as usual, taking money and handing out tickets. You know how many checkpoints there are on the road," he continued. "We stopped at Amirabad, and a group of heavily armed Pakistani soldiers ordered everyone off the bus. An officer ordered us to show him our identification cards. The officer scrutinized each I.D., and the Hindu men were put in a separate line. After the officer lined up all the Hindu men, his soldiers shot them in cold blood. It was terrible; I couldn't watch. Everyone was terrified, but the officer told the Muslims to get back on the bus. My legs were shaking so badly, I could hardly climb the bus steps. I am so sorry. I wish I could have done something, but there was no way I could save your husband's life."

All that Prova had left were her broken dreams and four little boys. She said, "He loved us so much. We were so happy. He worked so hard to provide for us. Now he's gone and I'm alone. How will I ever raise these boys by myself?"

It was not long after this that I had to decide who to send to Dhaka for training in the art of doll-making, so that the Heart House ministry could continue. I went to Prova and asked if she would be interested. Prova was excited about the idea, even though I explained, "You can't take any of your children to Dhaka. You'll be at school all day and there is no place at the YWCA for your children to stay. You'll be gone for two months. I'll take you to Dhaka and help you get settled. When you finish the program, I'll come back and get you. Do you think you can find someone to take care of your children?"

Prova thought perhaps a relative would keep her children for the training period. When she returned from her village, she was beaming. "Yes," she said, "the children's grandparents are willing to keep them. I thought the boys might be upset, but they are excited about staying with my parents." Prova could leave for training as soon as I completed the arrangements.

We flew to Dhaka, where I rented her a room at the YWCA, introduced her to the teachers, and settled her in for two long months away from friends and family. I have often wondered how Prova found the courage to venture so far from home. I can't look back, she seemed to say. I have a family to feed but no husband to provide for me. I'd better get busy and find a way to take care of my children.

When I visited Prova in Dhaka, the program director smiled her approval. "Prova works very hard," she said. "You chose the right person. She has an artist's hands." Prova used every spare moment to practice the sewing and painting techniques that required great concentration and precision.

When Prova completed the doll-making program, we flew back to Chittagong. I went on to Malumghat; Prova went to her parents' village to reclaim her kids. When she returned to Heart House, I asked how the boys had fared in her absence. She laughed and said, "I don't think they even missed me. They had so much fun at their grandparents' house that I had to drag them away. I think they would have stayed there forever."

Now that Prova knew doll-making techniques, she became my right-hand person at Heart House. Though barely literate, she stored an immense number of facts in her head. I gave her the responsibility of choosing and training a team. She had to select women already involved in the Heart House project who could learn the intricate steps of crafting dolls. She managed the doll team and eventually supervised the village women who crocheted and embroidered on a piecework basis. Keeping track of workers and materials was not an easy task, but she kept her own tally sheets and did a good job.

Eventually, MCH needed all compound housing for hospital personnel, and the Heart House workers had to find housing in nearby villages. Prova moved into a rental house in the nearby village of Cha Bagan (tea garden). She saved every penny she could and finally purchased a small mud house within walking distance of Heart House. She and her young sons were happy there. Her boys eventually attended the Bengali Christian School at Malumghat.

Prova remained spiritually aloof for a long time, but she

gradually warmed to Christianity. One day she surprised me by telling me that the local church officers were examining her for baptism. The Heart House "doll lady" had made a commitment to Christ and had asked to be baptized, all on her own.

When I needed advice or an interpretation at Heart House, I asked Prova for help. She had a knack for explaining things I found otherwise incomprehensible, like the circumstances surrounding Kanan, an obviously pregnant young Hindu widow who appeared at Heart House from a nearby village. Her husband had recently died, leaving her with two small daughters, a tiny piece of land, and a small bamboo house. She excelled at her Heart House training and was pleasant to have around. When Kanan finished her training we found work for her in a sewing project.

The closer Kanan got to her delivery date, the more nervous her co-workers became. Every time I walked through the door at Heart House, the tension was palpable. I finally drew Prova aside and asked what was going on. She looked at me and said, "You know that Kanan has two little girls, don't you?" I nodded my head yes. "But you don't understand what's happening, do you?" This time I shook my head. Prova said, "The reason the women are so concerned about Kanan is that she has no sons. She really needs to have a male child."

"Why?" I burst out. "What difference does it make whether her baby is a boy or girl?"

"It makes all the difference in the world," Prova explained quietly. "If she has another girl child, her property will revert to her husband's eldest brother; Kanan and the girls will get nothing."

How was that possible? Kanan barely had anything to start with. Why should she lose her home and tiny rice paddy to a brother-in-law? I shook my head in disbelief. Although it seemed terribly unjust, it was the law. Kanan's total destitution was not enough to change the law of the land.

After hearing Kanan's problem, my tension increased right along with the Heart House workers. Imagine our relief when we heard that Kanan gave birth to a healthy boy. She could keep her house and land. The property now belonged to this tiny baby who had secured his mother's inheritance without knowing it. The ladies clapped their hands in delight when Kanan returned to Heart House, and her radiant face revealed her own relief.

Almost thirty years later, Prova is still "the doll lady" at Heart House. When Christ said, "For you have the poor always with you . . ." (Matthew 26:11), was He looking into the future and seeing the homeless and destitute in ages to come? The ministry of compassion is as vital today as it was in His day. Christ ministered to the wretched, poor, diseased, and destitute of Palestine. And to some of us, He has given a similar ministry: the task of reaching out to the needy of today's world. We minister in Christ's name, and for the sake of His kingdom.

twenty-five

Precious Jewels

When I was a little girl, my favorite hymn was "When He Cometh," also known as "Jewels." The term "jewels" comes from Malachi 3:17, where Christ talks about His return from heaven to gather those who love Him, and take them to heaven. He calls them jewels.

When He Cometh

When He cometh, when He cometh to make up His jewels,
All His jewels, precious jewels, His loved and His own.

Little children, little children, who love their Redeemer
Are the jewels, Precious jewels, His loved and His own.

He will gather, He will gather the gems for His kingdom:
All the pure ones, all the bright ones, His loved and His own.

(Refrain)

Like the stars of the morning, His bright crown adorning,
They shall shine in their beauty, bright gems for His crown.

—William O. Cushing (1823–1902)

The passage in Malachi also speaks about God's "book of remembrance," where He writes the names of those who love, fear, and think about Him. I want to be a bright jewel in Christ's crown on the day He returns to take His children home. As people came to Christ in Bangladesh, I viewed them as precious jewels destined to make up God's heavenly treasury. What a bright crown He will wear when He gathers these jewels, trophies of His grace, in heaven! Won't it be wonderful to see men and women from every tribe and nation, raising their hands and voices in praise to God as they stand before His throne? Some of those precious jewels will come from East Pakistan/Bangladesh.

RANU (Little Queen)

Ranu is one of God's precious jewels. An attractive Bengali girl who lost her smile in the 1971 war, Ranu lived in a Hindu village twenty miles north of Malumghat. Her family owned a large, rambling mud house and farmed enough rice paddies to feed the entire family. Ranu's father was killed during the war. A paternal uncle took charge of the family property, including some valuable jewelry meant for Ranu's dowry. Somehow, in the confusion spawned by war, the jewelry disappeared. Without a suitable dowry, Ranu had no hope of marrying within her own social class. Anger and bitterness consumed her every waking moment. Having lost her father and her dowry, Ranu felt that everything of value in life had been snatched from her. She couldn't imagine that anything worse could possibly happen to her, but she was wrong.

While visiting hospital patients on the female ward, I first saw Ranu, struggling to walk while leaning heavily on a walker. Her condition completely baffled the doctors. Tests and X-rays revealed nothing wrong. But Ranu was slowly losing her ability to walk. Putting any weight on her feet made her cringe in pain. However, when I first met Ranu, she faced a problem far more serious than her physical condition. Emotionally wounded by all that had happened to her, Ranu may have thought she couldn't trust anyone. She let me talk to her, but there was no smile, no cordiality, no warmth in her response. I wanted to befriend her, but she wasn't going to encourage me one bit.

When doctors performed a biopsy on tissue from Ranu's hip joint, the pathology report showed inoperable cancer. Because the cancer was located deep within the hip joint, no treatment would help. The nurses taught her family how to care for Ranu before she returned to her village. Her cancer was a death sentence unless God chose to intervene.

Ranu's cousin, Badol, a laboratory technician at MCH, was concerned about Ranu's well-being; he asked Linda Short and me to visit her. One day during the rainy season, Linda and I drove my little car up the highway to see Ranu. We parked well off the road and walked to Ranu's village on an unpaved path slick with mud. The village was called Moodi Para, but we quickly renamed it "Muddy" Para. Linda and I finally located the big mud house where Ranu lived, set in the midst of brilliant green rice fields.

Ranu's family welcomed Linda and me warmly. Her sisters brought water to wash our muddy feet and the stained hems of our saris, and they expressed surprise that we had walked all the way from the highway on the muddy path. Ranu appeared genuinely happy to see us. I checked her hip wound and made sure that her sisters had enough antiseptic, dressings, and pain medication for the patient. Ranu's family was obviously taking good care of her. Checking on her health gave Linda and me a good reason to visit. When I asked Ranu if she'd like me to tell her a story, she accepted with delight. Unable to walk any longer, Ranu's life, confined to the four walls of her bedroom, had grown monotonous.

I drew a stack of flashcards from my tote bag and told Ranu the story of Christ and the two thieves on the cross. I tried to explain, as simply as possible, what Jesus Christ had done for her by dying on the cross. Ranu needed to know that she could accept Christ and go to heaven, but that rejecting His offer of eternal life would send her to hell. Ranu listened intently to every word and appeared to understand. I asked her to think about accepting Christ as her Savior, and she promised to do so. Linda and I prayed with Ranu and told her we'd visit again as soon as possible. We drank tea and ate sweets with Ranu's sisters before slipping and sliding our way back to my car. The fact that we had been so graciously received in an orthodox Hindu home was an answer to prayer. Linda and I continued to pray that God would open Ranu's eyes to the truth of the gospel and give her a desire to know Christ.

Badol kept asking us to visit Ranu again. The hospital wards were full, Linda and I were very busy, and it was hard to find time to travel to Moodi Para. But one day we returned to Ranu's village and talked to her about accepting Christ. I asked, "Ranu, would you like to accept Jesus Christ as your Savior?"

I barely got the words out of my mouth when she blurted out, "Oh yes, I would!" She asked Jesus to save her. Satan made it obvious that this victory infuriated him. As Linda and I bowed our heads to pray with Ranu, the entire household erupted in loud conversation. The confusion was obviously a satanic ploy to overwhelm Ranu's prayer. The sudden explosion of sound gave Linda and me a weird feeling, tangible evidence of the presence of Satan's minions. We rejoiced that God had snatched Ranu from the gates of hell. Now she was ready for heaven.

Ranu's body grew weaker, but her spirit gained strength. She still lived in a Hindu home, but God would take her to Himself in His good time. Linda and I saw Ranu several times after that. Sometimes Joe and Joyce DeCook accompanied us. Ranu loved it when Joe brought his guitar and we sang Bengali hymns together. God answered our prayers by taking Ranu to heaven before her suffering became too severe. One of these days, I know I'll see that sparkling jewel in heaven.

MRS. CHAKRABORTY

I suppose every country has its own names for foreigners. Each of us is familiar with the names used for foreigners in the United States, even if none of us would think of using them. Bengalis have their share of uncomplimentary epithets, too. A children's ditty, often heard by white-skinned missionaries, compares the foreigner's skin to the white of an egg. Because Bengalis have lovely, satiny brown skin, this is probably an apt description. Nonetheless, all of us dislike being called names, even in jest.

I had lived in Bangladesh for many years before I had a derogatory name applied to me in my hearing. When the inevitable finally occurred, it caused a nasty shock.

While visiting patients at MCH, I met a sweet Hindu lady named Mrs. Chakraborty. The doctors did not expect her to recover. During the time Mrs. Chakraborty was a patient, I had a hard time getting into the hospital to do my work because one of her two adult sons inevitably met me at the door with the request that I "visit Mother." If I had urgent business in the hospital, I had to use a side entrance so her sons wouldn't intercept me and shepherd me to her room. Several of the medical staff witnessed to Mrs. Chakraborty, and she was saved during her hospitalization.

I was thankful that God had saved her, but sending her back to a strict, orthodox Hindu home made me nervous. How would she fare spiritually? Her sons had not objected to her profession of faith, and I knew they would take good care of her at home. But I also knew Mrs. Chakraborty would be cut off from any spiritual fellowship as her life slowly ebbed away. Sometimes, Hindu families seem unconcerned when a relative confesses Christ. Perhaps they think it will all come right when the person is buried or cremated according to Hindu tradition; that the death rites will cancel out the earlier profession of faith.

A few weeks after Mrs. Chakraborty and her sons returned home to Chittagong, the DeCook family planned a trip to town. I begged a ride with them. When we arrived in Chittagong, we scattered in several directions, with Joe and Joyce carrying long lists of supplies they needed to buy, while I set out to visit my newly saved friend. The DeCooks and I agreed to meet at a Chinese restaurant for dinner before dark.

Since I once lived in Chittagong and spoke Bengali, I could find my way around with reasonable accuracy, and I was familiar with the part of town where Mrs. Chakraborty lived. Armed with her address, I hired a bicycle rickshaw and set off to find her. When the rickshaw driver reached the street where she lived, I told him I would walk the rest of the way. Since I wasn't sure which house she lived in, it would be easier to find it on foot. It was early afternoon on a bright, sunny day, and I was well accustomed to walking around Chittagong by myself, so I was not at all nervous.

I had not gone far, however, when a group of adolescent boys on the other side of the street began to chant. "White monkey, white monkey," they taunted loudly. In the twenty years I had lived in Bangladesh I had never been mocked like this. I ignored the boys completely, but I couldn't suppress a twinge of fear. Name-calling can lead to stone throwing—or worse.

Still not sure of my exact destination, I continued walking. Suddenly, a young, well-dressed Bengali man walked up beside me, matching his stride to mine. The rude chanting immediately ceased. The young man politely asked where I was going. I told him my friend's name, and he said, "I know where Mrs. Chakraborty lives. I'll take you to her house." He escorted me to the spacious house, spoke to a woman in the living room, then turned and left as suddenly as he had appeared. The woman immediately took me to my friend's (her sister's) bedroom. I could visit Mrs. Chakraborty, but only under the sister's watchful eye.

How could I talk to my friend of spiritual things while her sister listened to every word? Would I make life more difficult for her if I talked to her and prayed out loud? How could I make sure Mrs. Chakraborty was ready for heaven while this woman stood by her bed? *Help me, Lord; please help me,* I pled silently.

Just at that moment, the sister left the room. She was gone only for a few minutes, but that was long enough. Putting her hand on my arm, Mrs. Chakraborty looked me in the eye and said, "It's all right. He's in my heart. He's not going to leave me."

That was all the reassurance I needed. God would take care

of her, and I would see her again in heaven. I left Mrs. Chakraborty's house walking on air! Even if her family buried her as a Hindu, it didn't matter. God knows His own children. She was one of His precious jewels, part of His heavenly treasure. When God gathers His jewels, I'll see Mrs. Chakraborty again.

HANNA

Barisal is a breezy, surprisingly clean town on the northern side of the Bay of Bengal, an overnight ferryboat trip from Chittagong. Set like a jewel at the edge of the Bay of Bengal, Barisal boasts a series of channels that sweep the town's refuse into the bay. Lush, green coconut palm trees seem to grow everywhere, swaying gently in the sea breeze.

Riding in a rickshaw near the Barisal docks one morning, I heard a plaintive mewing above my head. Looking up, I discovered the trees were full of bats. In the daytime, these strange creatures hang upside-down from every tree branch. If a traveler stands on the deck of the Barisal ferry at dusk, waiting to leave port, he will see flying bats silhouetted against an apricot sky. The bats sleep during the day, but forage at night for food.

For many years Barisal hosted the Bengali language school for new missionaries, many of whom were British. The Bengali spoken in Barisal is very pure, perhaps because of the town's close proximity to Calcutta, India, where excellent Bengali is the rule, rather than the exception. Barisal is a center for higher education and offers many benefits to the young people who live there.

Barisal is also the site of the small, well-managed Oxford Mission Clinic and a large, impressive Oxford Mission church. Bengali young people who grow up in Barisal and wish to study nursing usually take their training at Chandraghona Hospital, established by the British Baptist Mission and located northeast of Chittagong. The Oxford Mission Clinic, while efficient and well equipped, is too small to offer nurse's training.

When Memorial Christian Hospital first opened, most of

our Bengali nurses were graduates of the Chandraghona Hospital nursing program. The hospital's professional and moral standards more closely matched what we expected from our nurses than did those of the government hospitals. Several MCH nurses from Chandraghona Hospital had grown up in Barisal.

While these young people attended the Oxford Mission church from childhood, the majority knew little or nothing of true Christianity. They were not Muslim, Hindu, or Buddhist, so they bore the label "Christian," even though they did not know Christ. They were familiar with Christian vocabulary, could answer questions about the Bible, and were surprised that anyone would suggest they were not Christians.

Sometimes these nurses told us that they were "born Christian," which seemed perfectly logical to them. If they were not Hindu, Buddhist, Muslim, animist, or atheist, what were they if not Christian? Their parents had grown up in the Christian church, and some had even suffered persecution. Didn't growing up in a Christian home make one a Christian? These young people were shocked to discover that the Bible viewed Christianity differently than they did. When we talked about such people among ourselves, we used the term "name Christian."

It was a delight to observe the Holy Spirit bring conviction to their hearts, as they learned in a personal way what it meant to accept Jesus Christ as Savior. As they heard God's Word preached and saw the lives of people totally committed to Him, they began to understand that being a Christian was a personal decision to love and follow Christ, not just a tradition of a religion claimed or followed by their parents. One by one, they became Christians, not just in name, but also in fact.

Among these young nurses were Ajit Sarder and his wife, Usha. A delightful Christian couple, they worked at MCH for several years before moving to Chandraghona. A few years later we heard that Usha had died in childbirth. We grieved for Ajit and his young family.

Sometime later, Ajit married Tunu, also a nurse. When they moved back to Malumghat to work at MCH, Ajit and Tunu Sarder built a house in nearby Cha Bagan and continued to raise their children.

At one point, Ajit brought his sister, Hanna, to Malumghat for treatment of a serious, undiagnosed illness. Testing showed that she suffered from leukemia. Although Hanna went through the agony of chemotherapy, she grew steadily worse. It looked as though nothing would stop the ravages of the disease. Her physical condition concerned us greatly, but her evident antagonism to the gospel disturbed us even more.

One day, Martha, one of the female Bengali evangelists, and I went to Cha Bagan to visit Hanna. Ajit's sister suffered from mouth sores, and her lips were stained purple with gentian violet, a dye that helps dry up the sores. By now Hanna was confined to bed, too weak to rise. Ajit and Tunu lovingly cared for her day and night. The day Martha and I visited, Hanna was openly hostile as we shared the gospel and prayed with her, even though she knew she might die. Looking into Hanna's eyes, it was as though I looked into the angry eyes of Satan. He held her tightly in his grasp, unwilling to let her go. Hanna's attitude grieved the Sarders, Martha, and me deeply; we were afraid she would die without Christ.

Just a few days after our visit, Martha and I learned that Hanna had accepted Christ. I was dumbfounded! God extended saving grace to her, and, weak though she was, Hanna reached out and grasped salvation. Hanna lived only a few days after her change of heart. Another bright, sparkling jewel entered heaven.

I will always remember Hanna's funeral. We walked across the rice fields to Ajit's home, where the family was preparing Hanna's body for Christian burial. As I walked into the yard, Ajit pounded nails into the cover of the plain wooden box that held Hanna's body. Ajit's young son, Tuhin, stood next to his dad, with tears rolling down his cheeks. He was handing nails to his dad.

Ajit talked to his son as he worked. "Tuhin, I know you're sad because Auntie has died. *Tap, tap.* If you believe that Jesus died for your sins, *tap, tap, tap,* you'll see her again in heaven. *Tap, tap.* That's where Auntie has gone. *Tap, tap.* She knew Jesus as her Savior, *tap, tap,* and now she's in heaven with Him. *Tap, tap.* You can go there, too, *tap, tap,* if you ask Jesus to take away your sins and live in your heart." *Tap, tap, tap.* The lid of the coffin was firmly nailed down. Ajit put down the hammer and took Tuhin in his arms.

Well, I thought, *if you want to teach a young son about salvation, death, and eternal life, Ajit has chosen an excellent way to do it.* I'm sure that lesson stayed with Tuhin for a long time. It has stayed with me for a long time, too.

These are just a few of the Bengali "jewels" with whom I expect to be reunited in heaven. I look forward to greeting many others, brothers and sisters in Christ. Some I knew in Bangladesh, others I've never met! But we'll all meet at the Father's throne—bright jewels for His crown.

twenty-six

A Fun Job

I hate to dispel a myth, but in addition to "fun jobs" missionaries tackle on the mission field, there are many not-so-fun jobs. One of my not-so-fun jobs was that of language coordinator. That's a euphemism for hounding people to complete their Bengali language study assignments, hand in their study sheets, and practice speaking Bengali. Despite the onerous tasks, I occasionally volunteered (or was pushed into) a job that turned out to be wonderful, joyous fun. Working with the MKs in music and drama was that kind of fun.

I'm not sure how it all started, but ABWE missionaries in East Pakistan tended to be musically inclined, almost from the start of the work. Probably only the "early" missionaries remember the orchestra that started in 1963 when a young Salvation Army couple from England arrived in Chittagong, their string and brass instruments in hand. Reg and Joyce Elliot attended the English church services directed by ABWE missionaries. This couple started, directed, and played in the orchestra. Those in the Christian community who played musical instruments contributed to the orchestra's magnificent sound. In those early days, musical evenings were a common social activity.

Many medical missionaries possess the wonderful gift of making music, and the ABWE family is no exception. Jeannie Lockerbie and Donn Ketcham, the soloists among us, sang often; Vic Olsen played the violin; Bob Adolph made his oboe and accordion sing; Reid Minich played a melodic baritone horn; and the rest of us filled in the harmony. Being gifted in music trickled down to the missionary kids, and that's where I got involved.

Having missionary kids with a wide range of ages on the mission field is a common situation. A group of families reaches the mission field at about the same time and . . . *presto*—you have a group of elementary school kids. The next time you turn around, they are all in middle school. About that time, a new group of missionaries arrives with elementary school-age kids, and so it goes. One of the challenges is finding music that everyone can sing. It was never a problem to accommodate various age groups in the Malumghat choir. At least choir members didn't *tell* me it was a problem until several years after the fact. One day, when all the MKs at Malumghat had become teenagers, Dan DeCook said, "Wow, is it ever fun to sing adult music for a change!" It suddenly dawned on me how gracious the big kids had been as they sang songs suitable for a much younger group of children.

Our first concerts consisted of music found in the MK school's music books. I'd pick a theme, then find as many suitable songs as possible. At Christmas I'd do the same thing, scouring the compound for music. I soon discovered that all the kids—well, *almost* all—really enjoyed singing together. Our one rule was that no child could participate in choir until second grade. Choir members had to be able to read. That way, they learned the words easily and could practice the music at home. We usually prepared two concerts a year, one for Christmas and one for spring, near the end of the school term.

Once the MKs reached high school age, they demanded heavier "stuff," and we sang musicals and cantatas theoretically beyond their capabilities. However, they always performed beautifully and enjoyed every minute of practice. Several developed excellent solo voices and went on to perfect their talents in college. I might have perspiration dripping off the end of my nose after an hour of directing, but I usually heard a loud collective sigh and the plea, "Let's sing it again." The MKs' appetite for music was insatiable.

I have forgotten the names of many of the musicals they performed, but I can never forget the MKs I directed and sang with at Malumghat: Olsens, Ketchams, Walshes, Beals, DeCooks, Golins, Adolphs, Eatons, and Staggs. Others joined us later, but these kids were in it for the long haul.

El Walsh or Barb Adolph provided accompaniment, covering my blunders and the choir's occasional false notes with their competent piano playing. As the children's expertise in playing piano grew, however, Lynda Adolph or Dan DeCook sometimes took over the job of choir pianist.

I was surprised at the way music "grabbed" the missionary kids. Lynda Adolph, returning from one furlough, said, "It wasn't any fun. American kids don't like the same things we do. They don't like to read, and they don't like to sing. They'd rather hang out at the mall." The Malumghat kids grew up in the jungle and entertained themselves, developing talents and skills that continue to enrich their lives. They certainly were not deprived children; their lives were filled with friends, laughter, and homemade fun. They didn't need TV or shopping malls to fill their hours.

When I left Bangladesh and returned to the United States, I received notes from several choir members thanking me for teaching them music. Michelle Beals, now a wife and mother, put it succinctly: "Music is the one thing in my life that has remained constant. I've moved several times, but music is always there, a part of my life. And it all started with choir at Malumghat."

We actually had some children who were labeled "tone deaf" somewhere along the line, but I didn't have to do anything about this. Peer pressure solved the problem. The kids on either side of the "deaf" children (who shall remain nameless), made sure the funny new kids learned to sing the right notes. I don't think they were poked, prodded, or stomped on. They just learned to go with the flow and sing what everyone else was singing. They certainly didn't remain tone deaf for long!

The choir worked hard at a cantata about the second coming of Christ. It was beautiful music and the MKs loved it. It had a rather shocking effect on the audience, however. Whenever I directed, I always smiled at the kids, encouraging them to smile while they sang. By the night of the performance, they always knew the music backward and forward, so it was natural to smile. But this night, they grew more and more solemn as the music progressed. Nothing I did evoked an answering smile. I couldn't imagine what was happening and, as director, I had my back to the audience.

When I turned around after the final number, it was easy to see what had happened. The parents were in tears! Donn Ketcham explained, "The combination of children's voices and words about the second coming of Christ . . . made the music overwhelming." Directing that particular cantata gave *me* goose bumps, but I didn't expect it to make the parents cry!

America's bicentennial celebration in 1976 called for a special program. The musical *What Price Freedom?* vividly portrays the incredible sacrifice the founding fathers made to purchase America's independence. The teachers at the MK school arranged for the choir to present the musical at the American School in Dhaka. The program included many hours of practice, sewing colonial costumes for everyone, traveling by chartered bus to Dhaka, and having lots of fun along the way. Teachers and kids both learned some previously unknown history, and we all gained a much greater appreciation of what America's freedom really cost.

The MKs and I also got involved with drama. I still can't imagine how it happened, because directing plays certainly wasn't anything I planned. The first time, it occurred almost by accident when the choir prepared a wild and wacky piece of music about a carnival, based on music from *The Carnival of Venice*. The music consisted of two different songs sung in counterpoint. The singers *really* had to concentrate. There were enough teenage musicians to carry the singing parts, and some of the younger kids decided on their own to work out a circus act. I had no idea what to expect, but they combined tumblers, dancers, and clowns with the music, to hilarious effect. It kept the parents and little kids laughing all evening. Maybe that's what gave the MKs the idea they could act—or perhaps it was because they were great hams anyhow.

The play that was the most fun was *You're A Good Man, Charlie Brown*. I held auditions for the major roles, but for the walk-ons and smaller speaking parts, the MKs decided what characters they wanted to portray. Dan Golin's excellent singing voice and quiet, gentle manner turned him into the ultimate Charlie Brown. Susannah Beals threw herself into the role of Lucy, teaching Linus all kinds of misinformation, with Lucy's typical assurance that she's right about everything. Ricky Adolph stole the show at the audition and—with his big blue eyes and beloved blanket—portrayed Linus to perfection. All the actors contributed just the right touch to make it an unforgettable performance.

How did each MK *instinctively* identify so perfectly with the character he played? It was almost scary! Did they actually possess the characteristics that Charles Schultz brought to life in *Peanuts*? They certainly gave me that impression—and they had some of the parents asking the same question.

One of my favorite characters was Pigpen, but for a very special reason. Tim Golin (alias Pigpen) was Johnny-on-the-spot every time we rehearsed our play at the Bengali school. The school's large stage was strewn with long, heavy tables and benches that had to be removed before rehearsal. I couldn't move them by myself, and it was April—a hot and humid time of year. Every single time, just as I arrived at the schoolhouse, Timmy roared up on his bicycle, a big smile lighting his face. He was just a little guy, but the two of us made short work of moving the benches and tables, getting the stage ready for our practice. His face, hands, and T-shirt were smeared with dirt for his role in the musical, but impish, smiling Timmy was my hero.

I recently attended a performance of *You're A Good Man, Charlie Brown,* staged by a college drama group. Instead of the young man performing Snoopy, I saw Kathy Stagg sitting on the doghouse singing "Suppertime," with her long floppy ears and black nose. And there he was—Charlie Brown (Dan Golin)—banging his head against a tree, while Lucy (Susie Beals) said with conviction, "Snow comes up, Charlie Brown. Snow comes up!" The college kids were great, but they didn't hold a candle to the MKs I know.

I really thought we had escaped performing a drama the year Kathy Stagg graduated from high school. I had just heaved a huge sigh of relief, when I found myself still on the hook. Kathy, in the process of working on her graduation program, sent me a note saying, "Aunt Mary Lou, I've found the *perfect* play for graduation. I know you'll just love it!"

I shook my head and groaned inwardly. It was really too late to start work on a play. How in the world could we get it ready in time for graduation? But I had to admit that the kids never let me down. A dress rehearsal might border on disaster, but the kids always came through on performance night.

That was a difficult springtime for several families. Marty Ketcham and Joanie Eaton were leaving Malumghat, heading for college in the U.S. Malumghat was the place they loved best, and they were struggling with the implications of leaving home, family, and friends; they knew their lives would never be the same.

The play Kathy showed me was the story of the life and martyrdom of John and Betty Stam, missionaries to China in the early 1900s. Casting, as usual, fell into place without a hitch. Kathy would play the part of Betty; Marty would be John, her husband. Joanie Eaton and Dan Golin were cast as Betty's parents, missionaries in a different part of China. Dave Ketcham was the pastor who married the attractive young couple. While these were the key roles, the rest of the kids filled important parts that pulled the play together—and punched the audience in the solar plexus.

Kit Ketcham made the beautiful stage sets, and other parents sewed costumes and found the necessary props. I really had little to do except to direct the rehearsals, making sure everyone learned his or her lines, and to pull all the pieces together. That proved to be a major challenge for this play. Joanie, in particular, struggled with her imminent departure for the U.S. The most commonly voiced comment at rehearsal from her peers was, "Joanie, *when* are you going to learn your lines?" I knew she'd learn them eventually, but right then she had trouble focusing on anything other than leaving home.

The play went off without a hitch, but it turned out to be another tearful evening. The most audible sound, other than the dialogue, was the sniffling of mothers in the audience. Being missionary mothers, they could easily envision the conflict with the communist bandits, which ended in the death of John and Betty Stam. Martyrdom still occurs today on the world's mission fields.

Near the end of the play, John and Betty kneel before their Chinese captors. A red light comes on and, just as the curtains close, huge blades fall on their necks. I was in the audience and heard the "thump" as Marty and Kathy fell forward, slapping their hands on the stage.

Joanie and Dan walked out to stand in front of the closed curtains. As Betty's parents, they told how God preserved their granddaughter, the baby girl John and Betty left behind. The communists hadn't found her; the Chinese Christians delivered her safely to her grandparents, a living trophy of God's grace, hidden from the carnage by God's omnipotent hand. Joanie knew her lines perfectly and was, for a few moments, Betty's mother.

After the play, Kit Ketcham, round-eyed with excitement said, "I heard their heads fall on the ground just as the curtains closed!" She shuddered, and I nodded my head understandingly. That's exactly what it sounded like to me, too.

It *was* a beautiful play, perfect for Kathy's graduation. I'm still not sure how we pulled it off. But MKs *always* come through in the crunch. Their singing, acting, and living out their lives in Bangladesh made my life richer and fuller by association. What fun to be a part of their lives, sharing their joys and sorrows, and claiming them as my nieces and nephews. A wonderful "fun job," and one I wouldn't have missed out on for anything!

twenty-seven

Acting Headmistress

While on furlough in 1980, I asked the Lord, *What do you want me to do when I return to Bangladesh?* I'm sure that many missionaries return to the mission field with a well-defined plan of action. But I had been involved in various ministries since my arrival in East Pakistan, and now I was uncertain of my future.

I had performed both medical and dental work at the hospital, but now Babul, the dental technician I had trained, did a good job in the dental room and seemed to enjoy the work. I had helped prepare Bengali literature for publication and worked with the Bible translation team, helping to check the colloquial translation of the New Testament. Then, after the war in 1971, I had shifted gears and become involved in women's rehabilitation at Heart House. Then Jimmie Nusca, a gifted seamstress, taught the Heart House ladies a variety of sewing skills and developed new items for sale. Jimmie was a big help at Heart House and capably managed the workshop during my furlough. *So, Lord, what do I do now?* I asked.

There was no clear word, no tug on my heart toward a new or different ministry. I would just have to wait and see what my Father had in store for me.

When I returned to Bangladesh, I learned that the Bengali Christian school at MCH faced a crisis. Several missionaries, concerned about hospital staff and local Christian children, had established the school in the early days of MCH's existence, when schooling in the area was scarce and sub-standard. The school at Malumghat provided high-quality Christian education for children of our medical staff, imperative if we were to attract and retain Christian nurses in this remote location. Christian education was an excellent tool for training Christian young people, as well as evangelizing the unsaved. Employee families were enthusiastic about the school's serious approach to education. The school committee expected teachers (and students) to attend school every day without fail. This was not true of local schools, which exercised a relaxed approach to daily education. If the teacher showed up, school was in session. If the teacher didn't appear, school was cancelled for the day.

I had served on the Bengali school committee for several years, and sometimes the task of helping solve school problems fell to me. The school had started with kindergarten and added one class each year. Now the school enrolled students all the way through high school. Teachers taught standard government curriculum, but because Memorial Christian School was not registered with the government, we transported our high school students to the nearest town for final examinations. Without that final exam certificate issued by the government, no Bengali could attend college or university.

Shortly after I returned to Malumghat from furlough in 1980, the school committee and Malumghat missionaries met to discuss the current problems. The committee had dismissed a national teacher for insubordination. When Vic Olsen, on behalf of the committee, discussed the situation with school parents, he discovered that they felt deep dissatisfaction with the way the school was being run.

Vic explained the problem this way, "The headmaster has done a good job up to this point, but he doesn't have a college degree, and the parents and teachers know it. The school has grown beyond Mr. Roy's ability to direct it.

"When we started our little school, we didn't need a headmaster with a degree in education. Our employees were young parents with small children. Now those children are teens in need of well-educated teachers and strong leadership. At this point, most of the teachers have more education than Mr. Roy. Because he does not have a degree in education, the parents feel he is not qualified. The parents want us to keep our educational standard high, and to do that we must hire a qualified headmaster. I think this situation led to the recent act of insubordination. We have to make some decisions soon if we want to retain the parents' confidence."

The school committee decided to divide the school into two sections: primary (kindergarten–5th grade) and high school (grades 6–10). Mr. Roy would direct the primary school, but the school committee needed to find someone else to direct the high school program. This person would also have to provide supervision for the primary school in order to placate the students' parents.

Where would we find such a person? Who had a schedule flexible enough to pick up another major job? We knew the parents would probably support a missionary in the supervisory position, as long as the missionary boasted a college degree. And there I stood, fresh off the plane from furlough, and at that moment uncommitted to a specific ministry. My college degree was in theology, not education, but nobody seemed concerned about that trivial detail.

In our school committee meeting, Vic Olsen suggested that I be appointed headmistress of the high school. Much to my surprise, everyone thought that was a great idea! I left the meeting in a state of shock. Was this what the Lord had in mind? I had been teaching for most of my life in one capacity or another. But could I direct the high school, keep 200 children and their parents happy, supervise a large Bengali teaching staff, and retain my sanity? From my vantage point, it looked like an insurmountable task.

When I asked the Lord about it, He was wonderfully encouraging. I insisted that the job was way over my head. The Lord promised to teach me Himself, and He reinforced the promise with the words of John 14:26, "But the Comforter, who is the Holy Ghost, whom the Father will send in my name, he shall teach you all things . . .", and 1 John 2:27, "But the anointing which ye have received of him abideth in you, and ye need not that any man teach you." He could teach me now; He had certainly taught me many times before. He promised to give me the wisdom and understanding I needed, one day at a time.

The Memorial Christian School committee met with the unhappy parents, explaining the decision on new school leadership. The committee stood one-hundred percent behind me, which was a great encouragement. The parents received our announcement with hearty approval. I apologized to the headmaster and the parents for the recent incident of insubordination. Then I expressed the committee's full support of Mr. Roy in his new position at the primary school and said that we expected the full support of the parents as well. I would take on the job of headmistress of the high school, and we would try to make Memorial Christian School a place of learning everyone would be proud of.

MCS met in two buildings. A long brick building with a raised platform at one end housed the primary school. The other, with mud walls and an asbestos sheet roof, housed the high school. There was also a small bamboo shack, used for tutorials, which housed a *big* snake above the woven bamboo ceiling. I avoided that building at all cost! The latrines were primitive, and the school had no running water. But the students, all from local villages, were used to primitive conditions. Facilities at MCS were far from fancy, but they were considerably better than those of most village schools in the area. This was to be my new kingdom, and here I would reign.

The walls in the primary school separating the classrooms were nothing more than army blankets, strung on wires. Mr. Roy told me that the little boys loved to jab each other through the blankets with sharp pencils. The high school's mud walls between classrooms left a wide gap between the top of the walls and the asbestos roof, providing limited ventilation on hot, humid days. The gap also resulted in unlimited noise from one end of the building to the other.

Most Bengali schools are "loud" schools, where children are encouraged to recite their lessons aloud. Students learn by rote, and the teacher knows who is studying by which students recite in the loudest voices. The noise level in both buildings was unreal! With that many decibels pounding their ears every day, the children should have been brain dead and deaf. How did the teachers cope with the volume?

I decided that the best way to know what went on in the classrooms was to teach in them myself. Teaching would be difficult for me because of the curriculum. To pass a government examination, the student must know *exactly* what is written in a given book. They must write *precisely* what the book says, or the teacher marks an answer incorrect. I didn't want to teach that way. Could I teach these children to think independently yet still enable them to pass the standard examinations?

The other high school teachers suggested that I teach 6th, 7th, and 8th grade English. I could teach the students reading skills and help them practice their English conversation.

I intended to teach English by speaking English in the classroom, a strategy that horrified the Bengali teachers. "No, no," they said. "You can't do that. None of the children know enough English. You'll have to use Bengali or they won't understand you."

"Let's try it," I suggested. "I won't know whether it will work or not unless I try. If it doesn't work, I'll try something else." The children were excited to have an English-speaking teacher. Their strong motivation to learn English made my job much easier. They wanted to learn "real English," and they worked hard at their lessons.

I introduced "praise papers" into my classroom with excellent results. If a student did the homework and got a good grade, he received a colored paper with a picture on it. I wrote the student's name and special achievement on the front of the paper. My students covered the walls of their houses with those papers. Parents told me that homework for my classes always got done first, because of the "praise papers." The concept of praise helped the students learn English, while improving their study habits at the same time. I was nervous the first time they took an examination, but they performed well. They were making steady progress and enjoying their English classes.

Almost twenty years earlier, Becky Davey and I had taught missionary kids while their mothers studied the Bengali language. We used Calvert School materials, which assumed the teachers were untrained. The MKs loved the curriculum and worked hard at their lessons. Now I was working with Bengali kids in a similar situation. I discovered that teaching children is pretty much the same, whatever their nationality. Teaching is both incredibly hard work and lots of fun!

For the first few months, I went to school each day shaking in my shoes. I was "acting" headmistress, in the truest sense of the word. Every day I put on an act. I was afraid that someone would discover how poorly qualified I was for the job, college degree notwithstanding.

My students were highly motivated and quickly learned the basics of English. The Bengali language is wonderfully regular. Pronunciation follows a set pattern, and idiosyncrasies usually have an obvious reason. Usually, that is, but not always. When I was studying the Bengali language, one of my teachers used to answer the question, "Why is this true in Bengali?" with the question, "Why is the sky blue?"

In the English language, changes in pronunciation do not follow any set rule, and many abnormalities are simply not explainable. I felt keen sympathy for these young Bengali students trying to unravel the mysteries of the English language. Learning Bengali is difficult; learning English may be even more challenging.

I found bribery to be a wonderful teaching tool. My students loved to sing. I taught them English songs to improve their comprehension and pronunciation. Every day they greeted me with, "Oh, Teacher, let's sing. Please, Teacher, please." So we sang the songs they enjoyed, but only *after* they completed the assigned lesson for the day. If they were rowdy or slow at their work, they didn't get to sing. Most of the time, they worked as quickly as possible, anxious to sing for a few minutes at the end of the hour.

I sang more with the younger children in the lower grades. The workload in 8th grade was so heavy that it didn't leave much time for fun, but I thought the older students wouldn't care. I learned how wrong I was when the older students chided me, "How come you *always* sing with the other kids and *never* sing with us? Don't you like us?" I had to include an English song in the curriculum now and then, just to keep the older students happy.

Classroom conversations usually sent me home laughing. The conversation often went something like this:

> NIDHU (7th-grade boy): "Oh, Teacher, it is so hot! I wish we had an electric fan in our room."
> ME: "Oh, Nidhu, I'm sorry. I wish I had enough money to buy a fan for our classroom, but I don't."
> NIDHU: "Well then, if we only had a tree to shade our room. That would help a lot."
> ME: "Well, Nidhu, I did plant some trees. But it will take them awhile to grow."
>
> *There is a moment of intense concentration as Nidhu absorbs this information. Then he says, "You mean those trees you planted yesterday?" And the room erupts into laughter. Then I walk up the aisle to check a student's work.*

7TH-GRADE BOYS: "What's that awful smell?"
7TH-GRADE GIRLS: "Oh, Teacher, you smell so good."

(Obviously, the "smell" the boys are complaining about is my cologne.)

Interestingly enough, this is the kind of comment I'd expect from 7th-grade students anywhere in the world.

During the five years that I worked at Memorial Christian School, God helped the school committee make some wonderful changes I could not have achieved by myself. To me, at least, the changes were phenomenal. I had been listening to Mr. Roy's complaints for years. Now I knew from experience how hot a classroom got without an electric fan. Having to pull wooden shutters over windows to keep out the rain helped me understand how dark a classroom got during the rainy season. The problems that had troubled Mr. Roy also troubled me. Now I was the one teaching with perspiration pooling behind my bifocals. The loud noise in the high school gave me a terrible headache. Suddenly, I had a vital interest in making changes in the school.

God supplied money for partitions in the primary school. A Christian youth group in the United States donated money for electric fans in the high school. The school committee found enough money to build the inside walls in the high school clear up to the roofline. A Bengali foreman suggested that we use brick interior walls instead of mud. This added several valuable inches to each classroom, because brick walls are thinner than mud walls. We eventually built a beautiful kindergarten, large enough to serve as an examination hall as well.

I was greatly concerned that the MCS high school students were exposed to cheating when they took their government examinations. Theoretically, a proctor expelled any student caught cheating in the examination hall. However, a proctor couldn't always tell which student was the cheater. Rita Roy, the headmaster's daughter and a high school student at MCS, returned from an examination one day, literally trembling. She stood by my desk and said, "Teacher, the girl sitting next to me took my examination paper to copy it. I didn't *dare* ask her to give it back. I was afraid that if I said anything, the proctor would expel both of us from the hall. I hadn't done anything wrong, but I didn't know what to do."

The girl eventually gave Rita's exam paper back, but the incident was upsetting. I hated exposing MCS students to situations like that. Besides, it was demoralizing for our students to sit in an examination hall and watch the other students openly cheat to get good grades.

The MCS school committee finally decided to try to obtain government registration. This would enable us to give all the high school examinations on-site, except for the countrywide final examination. In Bangladesh, high school students matriculate following 10th grade after taking a standardized examination in a designated center near their high school. If students want to go on to college or university, they must pass this exam.

Because I knew very little about school registration, I consulted Mr. Jalal Ahmed, Bangladesh's Minister of Education at that time. A longtime friend of ABWE and Memorial Christian Hospital, he was well acquainted with government protocol. I said, "Mr. Ahmed, even though I'm the headmistress of MCS, I don't know how to register the school. I need someone to help me take the right steps to register the school as quickly as possible." Mr. Ahmed was gracious and helpful, answering my questions and giving me advice. He carefully explained the registration procedure, adding, "Write me a letter, telling me exactly what you need." I told him that I'd go back to our office and type a letter on ABWE's letterhead. We made an appointment to meet again the following afternoon.

The next day, I presented my letter to him. Putting on his glasses, Mr. Ahmed read the letter, jotted a few words on it, and handed it back to me. He had written, "I know this school. It is a good school. Please register this school." Then he signed his name. I'm not sure I realized just then what a huge favor Mr. Ahmed did for me by signing my letter. In Bangladesh, the position of headmistress is prestigious. Working out the details of registration took me into many government offices, where I was received with utmost courtesy. Mr. Ahmed's signature was the golden key that opened many doors.

The paperwork for registration was exhausting. I researched old files and copied dozens of papers. Once I completed that job, the school faculty and I prepared for an inspection of the facilities. On inspection day, the inspector met our teachers, examined the school buildings, asked many questions, wrote in her notebook, and went away. In less than a month, the school committee received official word that the Department of Education had granted the school preliminary registration. An annual inspection would follow, but MCS had passed muster. Memorial Christian School received full registration a few months later. Officials in government offices told me that full registration usually takes several years and often is very expensive.

MCS students were involved in all the normal school activities. They had sports, *futbol* (soccer) being the favorite. They put on school plays, celebrated national holidays with speeches and ceremonies, and sat for endless examinations. Then they left. I enjoyed seeing them arrive as little tots, stringing flower necklaces in the spring sunshine. Before we knew it, they were rawboned, lanky teens, scared to death of final exams.

One thing still amazes me. When I first went to Bangladesh, I knew of few educated local residents. Rural children performed heavy chores at home. Sons and daughters looked after the family's meager livestock. Older boys worked in the rice fields, while little girls learned to be good wives and mothers—toting the youngest sibling on a hip was a good place to start. Many village children never had the opportunity to attend school at all. Others did not study beyond 3rd or 4th grade.

Once Memorial Christian Hospital began to educate the local young people, something wonderful happened. The children's aspirations changed; they wanted to be doctors, nurses, teachers, and laboratory technicians. They hitched their wagons to the star of higher education. Many of them found Christ through daily Bible lessons at school. Even the youngest learned Scripture verses, Bible stories, and songs.

It seems wonderful that so many of these young people are prepared to take Christ throughout the country, making a living as they go. This is something many of their parents could not have done. Most of their parents were poorly educated and made tremendous sacrifices to educate their children. My years in Memorial Christian School are full of special memories.

It's funny how God supplies our needs before we know we have them. As I had prepared to return to Bangladesh in 1980, one of my supporting churches had collected items they thought I might need. When I visited the church prior to returning, the pastor had said, "You *do* have room for these things in your baggage, don't you? Our church members would be very disappointed if you couldn't take them with you."

I assured the pastor that I would find room in my barrels for their gifts, and I shipped everything off to Bangladesh. When I opened my freight several months later, I couldn't believe my eyes. I had forgotten that most of the gifts that church had given me were school supplies: pens, pencils, colored paper, notebooks, and many other items I could use in Memorial Christian School. God probably smiled when I packed that barrel. He knew exactly what I would be doing when I got to Bangladesh. He had it all planned, waiting for my arrival.

twenty-eight

A Perfect Gem

After I left Bangladesh in 1985 to work at ABWE headquarters in Cherry Hill, New Jersey, I led a women's Bible study group at my church. This group of women had studied together for several years, enjoying one another's company. The name they chose for their group was GEM, an acronym with special meaning in their lives: *Grace Enough for Me.*

The class was composed of mature women, including two single moms. Abandoned by their husbands, they found making ends meet on just one income a difficult endeavor. A widow in the class coped with loneliness and the feeling that widowhood rendered her "invisible" in the church, a statement I heard from other "singles" in the church as well. One woman was a single schoolteacher, working in a public school. Others were divorced, fighting the stigma divorce brings in the Christian community. And I, their teacher, was a full-time administrator at ABWE. We all needed to apply God's grace to our lives each day.

I thought I knew quite a bit about grace until I went to the mission field. There I discovered that I still had a great deal to learn on this subject, and I had barely scratched the surface. Perhaps this was because I grew up in the era of "hellfire and brimstone" preaching. It was difficult for me to really understand how grace applied to me as a believer. I knew I was saved by God's grace, but what did I really know about the reality of that grace being active in my daily life?

Growing up, I was frustrated by what I perceived as a laundry list of do's and don'ts, which seemed to define Christianity.

There were things Christians did and things Christians did not do. In my thinking, doing the right things earned me God's approval. I actually felt, however, that the things on the "Do list" were more closely related to the approval of people than the approval of God. On the other hand, items on the "Don't-do list" seemed to be related to God's disapproval of my actions. I was afraid of God's instant punishment if I strayed an inch from the straight and narrow path.

This philosophy of fear-motivated service followed me through high school and Bible school onto the mission field. Conformity to a set of rules becomes almost second nature if you do it long enough. I did what was expected of me without giving it much thought. But beneath the surface, there were undercurrents of frustration and rebellion. I did not understand *why* they were there, but neither could I outrun them. I believed that God showed me His will for my life, and I did it to the best of my ability. Fear of being *zapped* if I stepped out of line, however, stole much of the joy from my Christian service for many years.

I had been a missionary for a long time before God brought this into focus for me. Work on the mission field was not easy; often it was downright grueling. I could work at the hospital twenty-four hours a day and still not finish all my work. I went home after every long, exhausting day, only to find another one waiting for me the next morning. Working all night in the operating room never erased the next day's surgical schedule. Other assigned duties were less strenuous, but placed equal demands on my time and energy.

An unusual strain of hepatitis periodically sent one or more of us in Bangladesh to bed with an aching liver. On one of these occasions, I was lying on my bed bemoaning the fact that I had read every book on my bookshelf numerous times. I picked up a little book called *Satan Is Alive And Well on Planet Earth,* by Hal Lindsay. Much to my surprise, I discovered that I had read only halfway through the book. *Happy day,* I thought. *I actually found* something I haven't already read at least three times.

I scanned the first part of the book to refresh my memory before starting a chapter called "The Guilt Trip." What I read in that chapter astonished me. The entire chapter addressed a specific lack in my life at that moment. What I needed, in order to see God's grace in its magnificent perfection, was the realization that God accepted me unconditionally. He knew my weakness, rebellion, frustration, and anger. And, wonder of wonders, God was not standing in heaven with His finger pointed at me. He was not waiting to *zap* me the moment I did something that displeased or disappointed Him. This was true grace. I can't tell you what a wonderful sense of release I got from this sudden explosion of knowledge.

I was so excited that I ran down the hall to nurse Alice Payne's room. I said, "Alice, you must read this. It is so wonderful. I can't believe how wonderful it is. Just look at it!" Alice humored me by reading the passage, discussing it with me, and sharing my enthusiasm. When I went back to my room, I searched for the Romans textbook I had studied in Bible school. I scanned it, looking for grace, then tossed it in the wastebasket. The writer of that textbook scarcely acknowledged the grace of God laid out in the Book of Romans.

It was after this watershed experience that I wrote a course on Romans for the women's Bible school program in Bangladesh. The concepts expressed in the Book of Romans were finally real to me. I was "accepted in the beloved," and I finally understood the meaning of God's grace as it applied to me. This was "living grace," grace sufficient for every need of my life.

Vital to our understanding of God's grace is the fact that joyful submission and glad obedience is possible only when we are overwhelmed by God's love, as seen in the sacrifice of Jesus Christ. Love accepts us unconditionally. Love does not wait gleefully for the opportunity to *zap* us when we stumble and fall. Love is the key to accepting God's gift of grace. And God's grace is expressed through His selfless love for His children. This was a totally new idea to me. It was all there; I just hadn't seen it before.

Knowing that God loved me unconditionally and accepted me "in the Beloved One," Jesus Christ, set me free to love and serve Him with great joy. I had no idea that service could be such a joyful experience. The hospital work didn't become less difficult; the days were still long and frustrating; and the weather didn't go from hot and steamy to balmy and pleasant. But I lost my terrible fear of being *zapped*. Wonderful, delightful, exciting freedom!

I discovered that I no longer needed long lists of do's and don'ts. God had placed in my heart the Holy Spirit, who desires and delights to teach me. Grieving God's Holy Spirit brought sorrow to my heart. Yes, the Ten Commandments are still in place; yes, we should keep God's law of love; yes, there are biblical standards that help us live for God's glory. But when we define the Christian life by a list, we stifle the Holy Spirit's voice and stifle our soul's growth. How can God teach and direct me if my eye is constantly on that ubiquitous list, rather than on Him? I don't believe He can.

God wants believers to be joyful. The New Testament is full of accounts of Christians' joy bubbling up in the most dreadful circumstances. Jesus Christ was joyful as He contemplated His return to heaven and Father, even though the way back to heaven led Him to the cross (Hebrews 12:2). Should we be any less joyful? The knowledge that He is with us every moment, and that He loves and accepts us without reservation, should flood our hearts with joy. And this joy should spill over into loving service every day that we live.

Jesus Christ also offers us His perfect peace (John 16:33). Knowing that He loves us and that His Holy Spirit dwells within to teach and guide us should quiet our restless hearts. One of the Holy Spirit's major tasks is to conform us to Christ's likeness while He prepares us for heaven. I truly believe that we can have an awesome impact on lives wherever we are if we truly understand what God's grace can do for us. He can provide saving grace, living grace, or dying grace, whatever the need of the moment. Grace includes salvation (free to us, but costly to God), unconditional love, counsel, companionship, and comfort—provided freely by the Holy Spirit.

I thank God for the day I learned that nothing I do can make Him love me less; nothing I do can make Him love me more. I have all of Him living in me right now. GEM really does mean *Grace Enough for Me*. All I have to do is hold out my empty hands and ask my heavenly Father to fill them with His overflowing grace.

Epilogue

How quickly the years have flown by. I spent my last five years in Bangladesh as acting headmistress of the Bengali Christian School at Malumghat. Working with the teachers and students at the school gave me five years of great joy. It was an enormous privilege to train Bengali children to live successful, happy, Christian lives. I also enjoyed encouraging their teachers to strive for high moral, spiritual, and educational standards for themselves and their students.

During this time, the Lord kept nudging me, saying quietly that this would be my last term in Bangladesh, something I found difficult to understand. Becky Davey planned to join me in my apartment in the Bengali nurses' quarters, and we looked forward to sharing a home again after so many years. Nonetheless, God made His will clear, and I had to accept what He was telling me. When I finally announced publicly that I would not return after furlough, everyone was surprised. Why leave now? Didn't I have even *one* more term left in me? I thought I probably did, but apparently the Lord had decreed otherwise.

When I returned to the United States in December 1985, I had no idea what I would do next. Wendell Kempton, then president of ABWE, encouraged me to consider a position at the mission headquarters in Cherry Hill, New Jersey. Me, sit behind a desk? I didn't think so! I had been free as a bird at Malumghat, wandering between the Bengali schoolhouse and Heart House. How could I stand the confinement of an office? Just thinking about it made me claustrophobic.

But when I sat with a group of men on ABWE's administrative team, and we talked over possible options, the Lord burdened my heart for the organization's single missionaries, scattered around the world. ABWE asked me to communicate with and encourage them. I'm not sure who encouraged whom, but I spent the next six years enjoying fellowship with the best group of singles in the world. I visited singles on their mission fields, and I learned to listen. Sometimes I listened to what the single missionaries, mostly women, actually said; more often, I listened to what they did not say. It was a special time of growth in my life, and I will always be thankful for the new dimension those years added to my life. The single missionaries accepted me like a sister and offered me the treasured gift of their friendship.

Working with field administrators proved to be a special experience. I was already familiar with Russ Ebersole's missionary heart. He had been Bangladesh's field administrator for many years. Now I was privileged to work with him and the other field administrators who bear the burden of ABWE's missionaries on their hearts. Though I was the only woman on that administrative team, the men accepted me graciously and offered me their friendship and esteem, special treasures indeed. The way those men loved, honored, and prayed for their missionary colleagues was indeed impressive. They wept with, and for, those who wept, and rejoiced with those who rejoiced. I greatly value the privilege of working with those godly men.

Then came the great exodus from New Jersey. Because ABWE was moving its headquarters to Harrisburg, Pennsylvania, and I planned to retire in 1994, moving twice in two years did not seem like a good option. Since my fellow administrators Art Cavey and Mel Cuthbert would retire in 1992, I followed their good example and left at the same time. We were praised and fussed over at our departure, but at least there were three of us to share the honors.

In September of that same year, I moved to central Indiana to be near my sisters, and I settled in—for a little while. Financial support from my home church in Rochester, New York, made it possible for me to do some special things after my early retirement.

Sheryl Liddle, a friend and colleague, and I were invited to visit ABWE's hospital in Amazonas, Brazil. So the year I retired, Sheryl and I flew to Bogotá, Colombia, and then down to Leticia, where we crossed the border into Tabatinga, Brazil. From there, a large riverboat took us to the Amazonas hospital. We traveled overnight, sleeping in hammocks, with people who spoke only Portuguese. What fun! We loved seeing the hospital and meeting the folks who live in considerable isolation along the Amazon River.

I celebrated my 65th birthday in Amazonas with the missionaries. Al Yoder, an ABWE missionary pilot, gave us an incredible ride back to Leticia in his little floatplane. Sheryl and I celebrated my birthday again with Lois Wantoch in Tabatinga, then flew back to Colombia. We stayed overnight with missionary colleagues, got on a plane for Florida, and flew through an immense double rainbow! We were in Orlando for my *real* birthday—celebrating, of course.

The Lord also graciously arranged two wonderful short-term trips to Bangladesh for me. The first time, I spent six months helping teach MKs at Malumghat and training new nurse's aides at the hospital. It was a special treat I enjoyed immensely.

More recently, I spent thirteen months at William Carey Academy in Chittagong, pinch-hitting for director Marilou Long while she and her family were on furlough. Talk about challenges! I was thrilled with the school, the students, the teachers, the missionary mentors, and the contacts with school parents. Everyone was extremely supportive, and my time in Chittagong was a special blessing. It was wonderful to make new friends, see former students ministering in various ways, and work with missionary colleagues. Those months will live on in my memory for a long time to come.

We can never go back and live our lives again. Probably, most of us wouldn't want to do that, anyhow. Pictures, old letters, continued communication with an extended missionary family, and precious memories all help bridge the gap between past experiences and our lives today. And Prova's gift—that beautiful gold ring set with a sparkling zircon—reminds me that God, in His infinite wisdom, continues to work out His perfect plan for my life, and that He is indeed worthy of our devotion and singlehearted service.

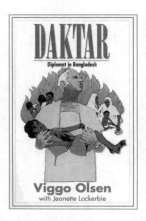

Daktar
by Viggo Olsen

The classic missionary story that continues to thrill readers with its exciting, inspiring account of Viggo Olsen, a young Christian doctor who helped establish the first modern medical facility in the new nation of Bangladesh.

Suggested Donation: $16.00
(includes shipping and handling)

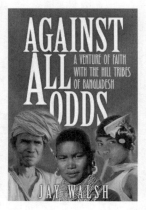

Against All Odds
by Jay Walsh

The engaging saga of Jay & Eleanor Walsh, who became missionaries to Bangladesh "against all odds."

Suggested Donation: $6.00
(includes shipping and handling)

NOW IN ITS THIRD PRINTING!

Interwoven
by Russ & Nancy Ebersole

Four years after the deaths of their mates, God led Russ and Nancy together and blended their families. *Interwoven* describes the many threads God wove together and recounts unusual situations they have experienced, such as a hijacking to communist China.

Suggested Donation: $15.00
(includes shipping and handling)

Port of Two Brothers
by Paul Schlener

The astonishing story of how God led and used brothers Paul & John Schlener to draw hundreds of indigenous people in an Amazon village to Himself.

Suggested Donation: $15.00
(includes shipping and handling)

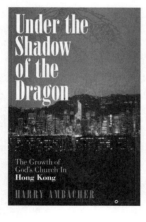

Under the Shadow of the Dragon
by Harry Ambacher

In the twentieth century, God used events in China and fear of the impending Chinese takeover to bring many Chinese people in Hong Kong to salvation. From 1965 to 1999, ABWE's ministry in Hong Kong grew from three small missionary churches to over 30 vibrant churches with Chinese pastors, transformed through the strategies of discipleship and partnering with nationals.

Suggested Donation: $18.00
(includes shipping and handling)

HOW TO ORDER

Write to:
ABWE Publishing
P.O. Box 8585
Harrisburg, PA 17105

Call toll-free:
1-877-959-ABWE (2293)

publish@abwe.org
www.abwe.org